The Enneagram

Carlos Mazuera

The Enneagram

The complete guide for writers, producers, film directors and screenwriters.

Literary Generation 2020

The Enneagram

The complete guide for writers, producers, film directors and screenwriters.

Carlos Mazuera

Editing and style correction: © 2023, Literary Generation 2020.

First print edition on Amazon: October 2023

ISBN: 9789962178170

Carlos Mazuera

"None of us is as smart as all

of us put together"

Japanese proverb

This book is for all people who want to know themselves.

To my teacher Carlos Enderle for all the knowledge taught about the Enneagram in his Personal Cinematographic Poetics workshop.

I always thank God for guiding me in the elaboration of this new line of high-content books called "New Experts", as well as my family, friends and colleagues.

Carlos Mazuera

Carlos Mazuera

Best Seller author nine (9) times including this book in English and Spanish: "Conócete a ri mismo y a los demás"; and the others books: "How to buy from Alibaba and sell on Amazon", "What the Married Hide", "IA and the Metaverse" and the collection: "You can lead to being a Nobel Prize in Literature"; Volume One, Two and Three.

Winner of the 2022 national contest "La piel escrita" micro-story category in Colombia.

Born in Cali, Colombia (1968). Panamanian citizen. Civil engineer. MBA at Kent State University, USA. Specialized at the Javeriana University, Colombia (Construction Management). He has directed more than 20 major engineering projects. Current Vice President of Research, Development and Innovation (R+D+I) focused on marketing and AI, artificial intelligence.

Specializations in US universities: Yale University (A Story for Our Times), University of Michigan (Writing and Editing), Wesleyan University (Creative Writing) and University of California (Academic English Writing Essay). Certificate in Literary Creation 2020 from the Technological University of Panama and the Writers Training Program (PROFE), novel genre 2020, essay 2021 and screenplay for cinema 2022 and 2023 from the Ministry of Culture of

Panama. Graduated from the Theological Institute by Extension (INSTE) 2022. He attended the Cinematographic Writing workshops and also Cinematographic Personal Poetics with the Mexican director, Carlos Enderle. He took courses at the University of Virginia (The Worlds of Historical Fiction), Duke University (Essay English Composition I), and Michigan State University (Script Writing: Write a Pilot Episode for a TV or Web Series). He took the workshop on Advice and presentation of film projects dictated by the filmmaker and producer Martha Orozco through the Ministry of Culture of Panama. Participate in various workshops with Altazor, Colombia. He is currently taking the Introduction to Film Production workshop with Carlos Enderle.

Founder of the 2020 Literary Generation group. Co-author of two books: "The world stopped, the stories continued" (Panama 2021) and "Among Friends Pure Story" (Panama 2023).

He is part of the anthologies: "Refuges and sunsets" (Ediciones PuertaBlanca, Argentina, 2021) and "Consummation of Eros" (Forum/workshop Sagittarius Editions, Panama, 2021) by Enrique Jaramillo Levi. He has published opinion articles for the newspaper La Estrella de Panamá.

Contact Links

Where do you buy other books by the author?

Social networking:

https://www.facebook.com/ElConstructordelasLetras

@MazueraCarlos

Instagram
@escritormazuera

Carlos Mazuera

Email

asturiaspluma@gmail.com

About This Book

This book belongs to the "New Experts" collection and its focus is that once you discover your true self through the Enneagram, you will be able to improve as a person and get to know others better. It is not oriented towards an awakening or spiritual growth filled with freedom and joy, a kind of "conversion". It is only a tool to help solve the problem of humanity, the lack of self-knowledge; but not to provide the means of salvation through self-discovery.

Although the Enneagram mentions the main passions as a limitation of the personality type, the main passion is not something inevitable and is personal responsibility. If that passion is caused by personality as the Enneagram suggests, even if we improve at compensating by cultivating the opposite personality, this will not give us redemption.

For example, for Christians, through repentance and conversion, Christ gives redemption by revealing the truth about man and giving the grace to be fully human. The Enneagram is just a method that helps us discover ourselves.

This book is for you if...

1.   You want to create complex characters for novels or scripts for fictional feature films.

Over the years, I realized that the vast majority of series and movies have had a great scriptwriter who knows very well how the enneagram enneatypes work. Now I write scripts with very complete characters in their thinking, saying and acting.

2.   Your goal is self-development and self-understanding, not salvation.

You realize your deeper values and reasons that interfere with abundance and inner harmony. You will learn to fully accept yourself and appreciate what is in you. This book will become a high-speed elevator to a new level of consciousness.

3.   You want to understand others and improve relationships.

The Enneagram speaks of deep motivation, the unconscious reason for people's behavior. You will understand what your partner wants, what the children need; you will find an approach to colleagues and family. You will learn to speak to be Heard

4.   You need a proven tool for the job.

The Enneagram is used throughout the world in business, team building, and counseling. You will get an advantage when it comes to communicating with clients in any activity: coaching, HR and sales. You will value time, efficiency and practicality.

As a result, you will get:
Reach a new level of consciousness. Realize your true needs, values, mental errors, strengths. Access a special resource state and balance emotions, body and intellect.

Improve communication and relationship. Find a way to negotiate with anyone. You will understand the true reasons for the behavior of loved ones and reduce the number of conflicts due to misunderstandings.

Master the diagnostic tool. You can read the interlocutor's meta-message and help him get what he wants. You will learn what is key for the client and you will respond quickly to their requests.

By the end of the book, you will be able to:

Improve the descriptions, performances, dialogues and wishes of the characters in your script. It will be of great help to the film director if, from the script stage, the character is complex and coherent between what he says and what he does. The producer may be more comfortable with the production of the film.

Understand how your personality works. Why is your life going the way it goes? And where to look for your internal resources to influence life and not get carried away.

Understand the causes of family conflicts. You will manage them and create an understanding and supportive environment for your children and loved ones.

Accurately identify the strengths of employees, stimulate them appropriately and build an effective team. The Enneagram has, for a long time, helped well-known campaigns with this. Speaking the same language in any people-related profession and selling customers exactly what is valuable to them: resolving objections quickly and easily.

Carlos Mazuera

The Enneagram

Index

Characters analyzed from Series and Movies

1. Game of Thrones.

2. Star Wars.

3. Scarface.

4. Friends.

5. Billions.

6. Twilight.

7. The Walking Dead.

8. Outlander.

9. Naruto.

10. The Simpsons.

11. Greys´s Anatomy.

12. The Lord of the Rings.

13. Gladiator.

14. Harry Potter.

15. Ertugrul.

16. Betty the Ugly.

17. Money Heist.

18. Fast & Furious.

19. Biblical characters.

INTRODUCTION

Know yourself

Before beginning, I will explain what the icons that you will find on the left margin consist of, whose function is to guide you through the book:

 This icon tells you that there is a recommendation or tip to keep in mind.

 This icon indicates the advantages of the topic addressed.

 This icon tells you the drawbacks to be aware of.

 This icon alerts you that there is technical language which you must learn.

 This icon informs you that there is a lot of valuable information content and that you should take notes.

 This other icon shows you an example as a guide to clarify the issue.

Now let's get down to business.

The Cherokee were one of the peoples who were grouped into the so-called "Five Civilized Tribes." Always known for their rich culture, their language and their traditions, they are undoubtedly one of the native references that has had the greatest impact on Western society.

One of the stories that has transcended the most is the Cherokee legend of the two wolves. The story is articulated as a lesson in wisdom from an old man towards his grandson. The first explains that, inside him, as in the hearts of all men, a terrible battle between two wolves breaks out every day.
Those two animals symbolize two opposing forces. One is evil, the old man tells his grandson. It is anger, it is envy, greed, arrogance and even sadness, the feeling of inferiority and ego. The other force is kindness, it is joy, love, hope, serenity, humility, compassion and of course peace.

When the young Cherokee asks his grandfather which wolf is going to win that battle, most of the stories that have come down to us through the media are answered with the following statement: **the one you choose to feed will win.**

 The word enneagram comes from the Greek ennea "nine" and gram "image." It is a modern dynamic model of personality development. The Enneagram is a powerful guide to self-discovery and development, as long as it is not used for value 

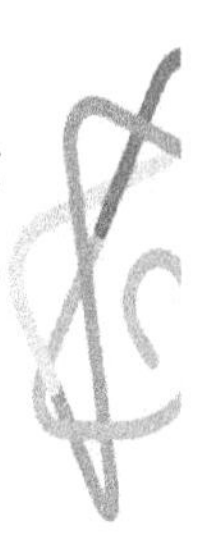

judgments and complacency. The use of the Enneagrams along with coaching enriches both models, especially with regard to personal development.

The uniqueness and high efficiency of the model is explained by the fact that it reveals the deep motivation of each type, stimulating personal growth. By working with a person's unconscious beliefs and values, the Enneagram allows them to be used as a resource.

 **The Enneagram will help you to:**

1. Create deep and round characters for writers and screenwriters.
2. Increase sales by learning more about your collaborators and clients.
3. Increase professional and emotional competence.
4. Improve your relationship as a couple.
5. Develop your own leadership style.
6. Work with basic unconscious emotions: fear, shame and anger.
7. Communicate better, say what you want to say, feel that you are understood.
8. Carry out Coaching of human resources consultants.
9. Develop behavioral flexibility.
10. Take that step you want so much to change jobs.
11. Solve a series of problems in the field of communication.

12. Understand the strengths and weaknesses of family, friends, and colleagues.

13. Recognize the possibilities of self-development.

14. Find out why you always fail at the same thing.

15. Know why you react explosively to certain people.

16. Understand what leads you to always find the same type of partner.

17. Feel better and eliminate that constant feeling of stress.

18. Find solutions and techniques to be more aware.

19. Develop skills to change what you think should change.

20. Discover factors that acted in your childhood and that are reflected in adulthood.

Although there are authors with a more recognized voice in the world of the enneagram, there are differences of opinion and beliefs among them. As I mentioned before, the Enneagram does not dictate giving up your spirituality or personal faith and adopting that of an Enneagram expert.

Methodology:

There are two methodologies to use when reading this book. The first, if you want to analyze yourself as a person and others. The second is by getting into the role of the character to be created in the novel or film script and beginning to complete it with the guide of the different chapters of this book.

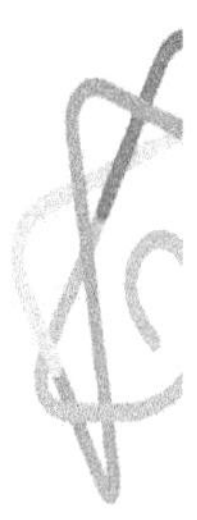

The Enneagram offers a journey of self-discovery that will lead to greater self-understanding and acceptance. Each of us has a key driving force, a preferred set of strategies, a unique compendium of talent that we can truly be proud of. Each of us sees the world and time differently. We are attracted to certain trends, habits and practices, while others are automatically avoided.

Ichazo did not provide character type descriptors, but only diagnoses and concepts as recorded by Charles T. Tart in his book "Transpersonal Psychologies." (Tart: 1975).

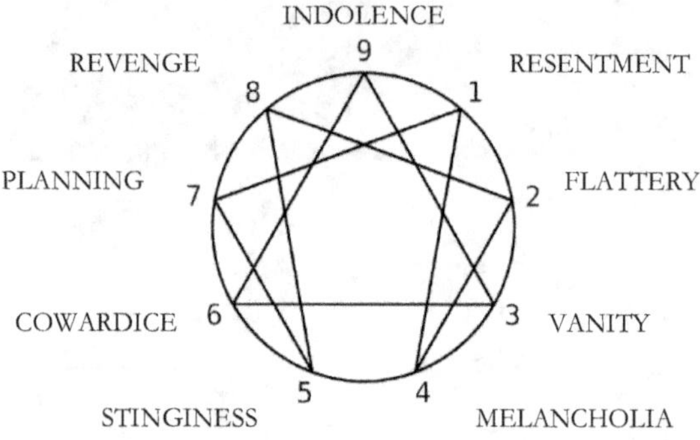

Perhaps your goals change and desires, strengths and new opportunities appear to expand your world map, reflecting the systemic nature and ecology of ourselves and the world in which we live. Today, with the help of the Enneagram, we will get closer to the content of our thinking: this is exactly the place where we get hooked, and here is the whole story of our life, habitual ideas, anxieties, disappointments and fears.

Each one of us has experienced life dramas, we believe in them and we are impregnated with them. The Enneagram gives us the opportunity to enter this realm and explore our inner world. Allow yourself to accept the invitation and travel without falsehoods, from the position of a neutral observer. It will help you separate judgments about people from judgments about their actions.

The uniqueness and high efficiency of the model is explained by the fact that, unlike other typologies, it is not limited to describing behavioral strategies, but reveals the deep motivation of each type. By working with a person's unconscious beliefs and values, the Enneagram allows them to be used as a resource.

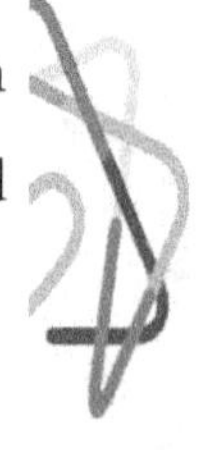

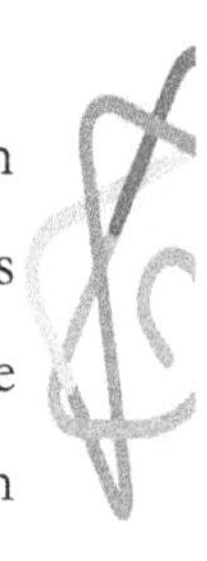

We will study nine specific types of thinking, and each of them corresponds to a certain way of managing one's own experiences with their related questions and comments. In addition, they are associated with ideas about figures that personify power with paths to success.

The Enneagram is not a way to classify or label people. The uniqueness of the Enneagram is that, by describing the general patterns, it speaks to the uniqueness of each one. According to this model, there is no better or worse type, there are nine different ways of being in the world, which is why it is sometimes so difficult for us to understand each other. It also describes the radical changes that occur in a person in situations of stress and comfort, reveals the principles of interaction between types. Internal dialogues are based on something very significant to us, in its essence something that has to do with our survival.

For example, these are dialogues focused on questions about:

- "Do they value my sacrifice?"
- "They love me?"
- "Should I help others more?"
- "Do I think I'm always right?"
- "Am I strong enough?"
- "Am I permissive?"
- "I succeed?"
- "I am safe?"
- "I'm comfortable?"

The fact is that this kind of internal dialogue binds us and "freezes" us in place, stops our movement and development. It's such an obsessive way of thinking that it holds us back because it interprets our life for us. We are busy fulfilling the roles imposed by them, and instead of life, we "play life", we get involved in a variety of games.

Games take someone into the world of management, control and power, the world of fame and success. Many of us very seriously play games that give a short-term feeling of joy and happiness, for example, the popular "board" game in the family, or aesthetic games, or the philosophy game, or business games.

No matter how enthusiastically we play, many of us are faced with the fact that our whole life is fraught with despair, and often even very strong and powerful games lead to a state of dissatisfaction and suffering. Knowing this, you can take a fresh look at the roles and rules that children inherit from their parents, and become something we inadvertently aspire to.

Today, the Enneagram model is successfully used in their work by Avon Products, IBM, Boeing, General Motors, The DuPont Company, Mitsubishi, Alitalia Airlines, KLM Airlines, Kodak, Hewlett Packard, Toyota, Procter & Gamble, Apple, Reebok, Motorola, Sony, American Press Institute, Coca Cola and many other companies.

If you want to get to know yourself better and understand more clearly the differences between each other, the Enneagram has a lot to offer you. It also serves as a tool for our personal, work and community relationships.

There are many people who have rigorously researched the Enneagram, many of them psychologists, analysts, business coaches, and therapists, and I think it's wise to open ourselves up to valuing their work and learning from them. The Enneagram is not the only method, here are two others focused on personality analysis:

The Egograma

The Egogram is a psychological test developed by psychologist Dusay based on the theory of interaction analysis. Based on the three ego states of C (infant ego), A (adult ego) and P (parent ego) from the interaction analysis, five personality types are diagnosed. It is one of the personality tests based on the theory of psychological research.

The StrengthsFinder

Strengthsfinder is also one of the personality tests often used in business. StrengthsFinder was developed by Gallup in the United States. If you answer 177 questions in the web test format, you will know your own strengths. More than a personality diagnosis, it is used as a self-diagnosis tool to know one's own strengths.

In recent years, the Enneagram as a tool for corporate coaching has become increasingly popular. One of the reasons why famous domestic and foreign companies have adopted the Enneagram is that it leads to the revitalization of the organization. By using the Enneagram in your business, you can improve human relationships in organizational development.

Listen to your inner dialogue... The Enneagram will help you. Remember, there is no "right" way to look at the Enneagram.

"What is the danger of the enneagram? Take it too seriously. " – answers Suzanne Stabile– "The enneagram is nothing more than a model."

In the following QR code, you can see how the 9 types of personalities behave during a dinner. Taken from gastroactitud.com:

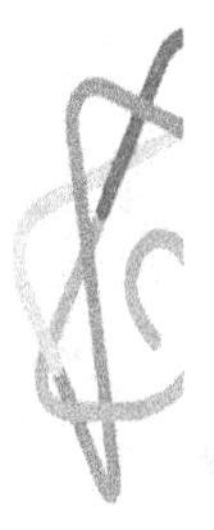

HISTORY

History of the Enneagram of Personality

The Enneagram is a description of the nine basic personality types and their relationships, based on a geometric figure. According to this method, there are nine main characters, as opposed to Sheldon's three, Hippocrates' four temperaments, and Lowen's five bioenergetic types.

As I mentioned before, the Enneagram is a figure with nine points arranged in a circle. Each of those points represent nine types of basic personalities. For this technique, personality can be understood as a set of relatively stable patterns that an individual presents: the reformer, the helper, the winner... And each "model" is assigned a number. The symbol dates back to Pythagoras and was introduced to the West by George Gurdjieff (1872-1949) in the 1900s.

Oscar Ichazo is considered the founding father of the method of describing character types and their interactions through the enneagram. Ichazo founded an institute in Arica, from which one of his students, Claudio Naranjo, continued the process of developing the Enneagram and brought it closer to our modern understanding. But, unlike the teacher, Claudio had medical training and was a psychiatrist. Naranjo spread it in universities such as California, Berkeley and Loyola in Chicago, thus knowledge of this concept reached the Jesuits.

The enneagram was popularized worldwide after the appearance of the book The Enneagram by Helen Palmer in 1988. Others of its disseminators are Don Richard Risso, Russ Hudson and Robert Ochs.

The enneagram is not scientific, because if it claims to be a method of diagnosing human behavior, then it should be able to demonstrate its effects empirically. To be a scientific theory, it would need that said technique has been or can be verified, reviewed and or published and that its methodology be normalized by scientific criteria, that is, that it has reproducibility, falsifiability and corroboration.

Sheldon supposes grading the proportion of each person's temperamental components from one to seven; However, it corroborates that these can be present in different degrees and combinations. (Sheldon, 1942).

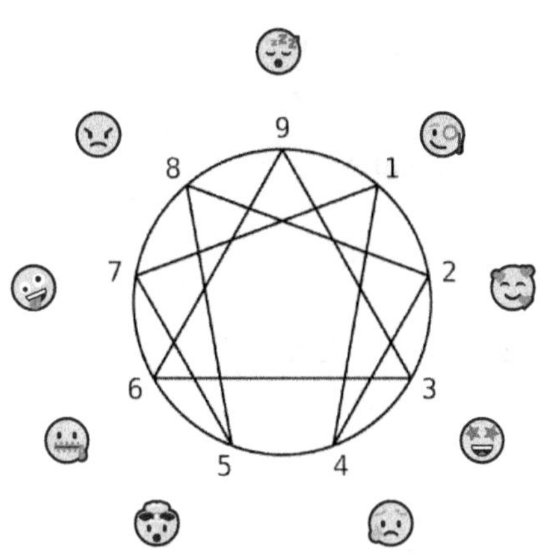

 **What the Enneagram is not**

Before you start studying the Enneagram of Personality, you should be clear about what the Enneagram is not:

1.   It is not a system of classifying people.

2.   Your enneatype has nothing to do with being a better or worse person.

3.   It does not tell us what or who we are, it only describes our behavior.

4.   It is not religion. Far from it a method of spiritual salvation.

5.   It doesn't nullify your individuality. It only indicates behavioral trends.

6.   The Enneagram is not the stereotypes with which enneatypes are described. There are no two people alike in the world.

7.   It is not a perfect model.

 Intellectual Mind

 Emotional Mind

 Instinctive Mind

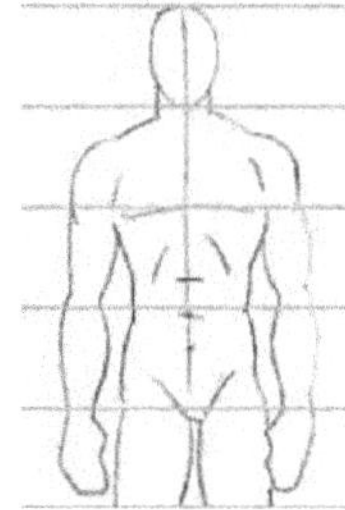

 The Enneagram describes three basic ways of thinking: the Intellectual Mind, the Emotional Mind, and the Instinctive Mind, which are represented respectively by the Head, Heart, and Body Centers.

Each of the nine personality types belongs to one of these centers. This means that each type is governed by emotions, instincts or reason.

Although we use all three centers in life, one of them is more developed. It depends on the leading center what is important to us in life, what we pay attention to, how we make decisions and what is worth working on the path of personal development.

According to Don Richard Riso, "Triads are important for transformation work because they specify where our main imbalance is; They represent the three main groups of ego problems and defenses, and reveal the main ways in which we contract our perception and limit ourselves. (Riso: 2000).

TRIADS

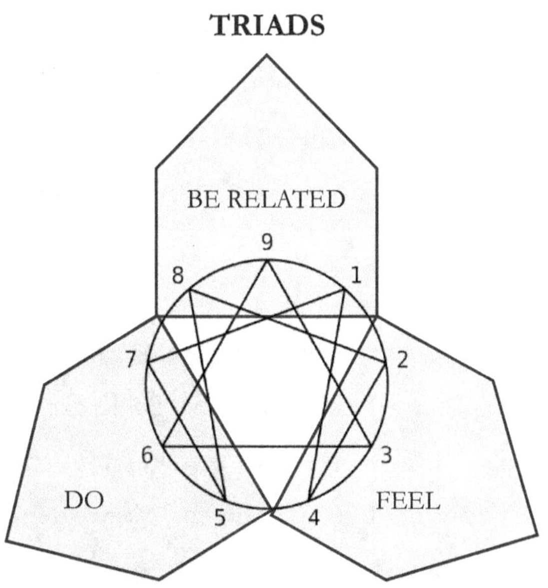

Center of the body - Triad of Relating

Sensitive Triad Who am I? What is my dignity?

Focuses on integrity.

The Gut Triad

Types of instincts - Types 8 - 9 -1

For these personality types, the use of the instinctive mind is characteristic. These types are very capable of sensing their body's impulses and acting spontaneously.

The instinctive center allows them to perceive the world in a natural, spontaneous way. They also support vitality and energy. The main problems are related to anger - aggression - self-control.

Type 8:

Control - aggression. Attention is directed to the outside world, to your environment. They want to control every situation and do not want to be controlled by others. They set clear boundaries and keep others at a distance. They repress their own weakness and constantly "fight" to be "the strongest. " Anger is directed outward.

Type 9:

Control - passive aggression. Attention is directed both inward and outward. They avoid anything that could disturb their peace and tranquility. They repress their own impulses and act passive-aggressively towards the environment. Very often they remain passive: they suppress their own anger.

Type 1:

Control - aggression. Attention is directed inward, to internal impulses. They control their own emotions, allowing only a small amount to spill out. Self-control in relation to your own "unnecessary" impulses. Resistance to external factors. Anger is repressed.

Heart Center – Triad of Feeling

Sentimental Triad How much am I worth?

It is based on attention

The Heart Triad

Emotional Types - Types 2 - 3 - 4

These personality types are characterized by the use of the emotional mind. This type is good at focusing on other people, establishing personal contact with them, and thus finding

himself.

The emotional center allows us to build a natural identity and is responsible for healthy self-esteem, as well as adequate appreciation and respect for other people. The main problems are associated with shame - hostility - comparison - self-identification - image - positive feedback.

Type 2:

Self-identification. They direct attention to the outside world, to other people: "I want them to need me." A person's self-identification is based on how others evaluate me, on their positive feedback. Very attentive to others, helps to earn approval. Shame is suppressed by the feeling that you are needed.

Type 3:

Image - competition. They direct their attention both inward and outward. In people, the 3rd type has strong internal images of success "I am successful", "I look as if I have already achieved the goal" and at the same time it is important for them that others highly appreciate their achievements. "I am admired for my achievements. " Shame is subconscious and repressed.

Type 4:

Self-identification - Comparison. Direct attention inward. A sense of self-worth and transcendence is acquired, based on internal ideals. Personal identification is based on emotions, fantasies and previous events. They construct identity through the experience of uniqueness: "Who am I if there is no one similar around me? If I am truly unique, the shame will disappear." At the heart of unpleasant experiences is the belief that "I am not like others": they experience an extremely painful feeling of shame.

Center of the Head – Triad of Doing
Conscious Triad: Will I be able to sustain myself in life?
It is based on Trust
The Head Triad

Types of Intellectual Mind - Types 5 - 6 – 7

These personality types are characterized by the use of the intellectual mind. They have exceptional abilities to think, plan, analyze and generate ideas. They love gathering knowledge and having intellectual discussions.

The intellectual mind allows us to experience inner guidance and direction, thus creating a sense of security. Main problems are related to fear - avoidance - planning - internal dialogue - support - feeling of security.

Type 5:

Fear - Planning. Direct attention to the outside world. They perceive the world as dangerous and unreliable. Trying to understand and manage the world –"I don't have enough knowledge to know the practical side of life." Constantly looking for a place where they can feel safe alone with their introspections –"In my thoughts I am safe, they support me." Fear is fully realized.

Type 6:

Analysis - Doubt. Direct attention to the external and internal

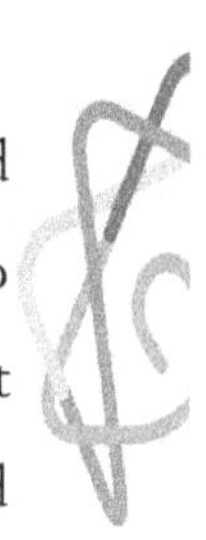

world. They experience anxiety about their own insecurity, and at the same time doubt other people's intentions. They strive to receive support and guidance from authorities and beliefs, but at the same time they do not dare to trust them. Fear is suppressed and mostly unconscious.

Type 7:

Ideas - Planning. They turn their attention inward and, in their minds, perceive the world as a place full of possibilities. They try to compensate for the feeling of inner dissatisfaction by distracting themselves with entertainment. On a subconscious level, they are afraid of being alone with themselves, of facing their inner anxiety. Fear is suppressed by avoidance.

WINGS

The nine types of the Enneagram are connected by a circle. Because of this connection, each type is more or less influenced by its neighbors. This is called wings.

For example, Type 1 may have some inherent characteristics with Type 9, resulting in Type 1 tending to be more comfortable, a bit lazy, and not as perfectionist in all aspects of their life. The anger becomes more hidden.

Also Type 1 may be more strongly influenced by Type 2 because that person begins to pay attention to people's needs. It becomes important to him.

ARROWS

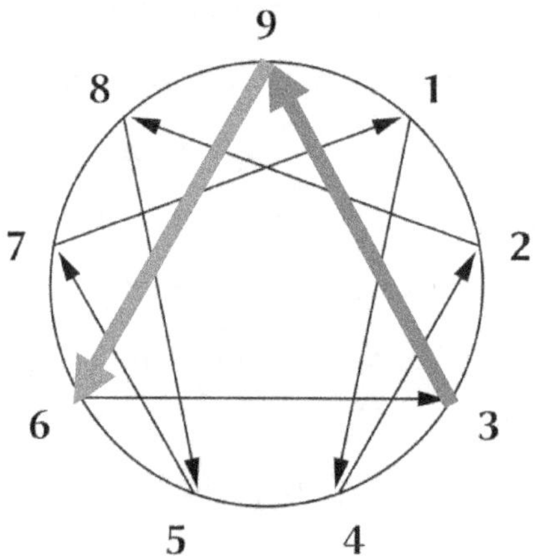

The Enneagram describes and explains the changes that occur to us in stressful situations, when we are under pressure and insecurity, as well as in situations in which we feel confident and secure.

When we are in a state of trust and security, we have the power to "swim against the current" and move against the arrow: we access resources of the kind from which the arrow comes. This positive development increases our comfort zone.

On the contrary, when we are under pressure for a long time (for example, difficult relationships, problems at work or emotional problems), we become weak and do not have enough strength to withstand difficulties. We go with the flow and acquire

characteristics of the type indicated by the arrow.

Let's look at an example: if a type 9 person feels confident and secure, then they move to type 3 and become more efficient and determined. He is focused on the result and on himself.

If a type 9 person is under prolonged pressure, then he begins to move towards type 6 and becomes more skeptical, begins to doubt himself and those around him.

 Now you are going to do your own test, but when you start to know the different types, you must avoid quick conclusions like this at all costs:

- Don't miss a button on your clothes, he lets you know. He is a Type 1.

- Whenever I look at her, she has a smile. He is a Type 2.

- Every time I see him, he is well groomed and perfumed. He is a Type 3.

- That person, who always wants to attract attention, is a Type 4.

- I went to hug him and he stretched out his hand like a bridge. He is a Type 5.

- The line has been stopped for a while because he can't decide what to eat. He is a Type 6.

- He is the entertainer of the parties. He is a Type 7.

- He got really upset, he's a Type 8.

- He spends all day playing on his cell phone, disconnected

from the world. He is a Type 9.

 There is no single "official" test to determine the enneagram of personality. The developers of these tests do not recommend that children under 14 years of age take them, and those under 18 years of age should do so under adult supervision.

I leave you the link to a page where you can take the test and know which Ego you are:

 https://enneagram-personality.com/en

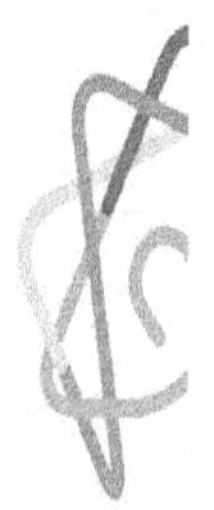

THE REFORMER

Idealist-Perfectionist
Enneatype 1

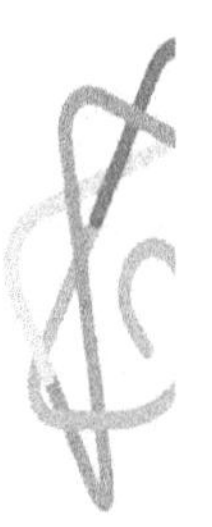

"To understand the Enneagram, you have to imagine it in movement… without movement it is a dead symbol…"

George Gurdjieff

Perfectionists are idealistic, principled, ambitious, respectable, orderly, reliable, loyal, and punishing. They tend to think in a coherent, polarized or black or white way, good or bad, right or wrong, which creates rigidity and lack of flexibility.

Type 1s are demanding about what they do and strive to get closer to an ideal version of themselves. They have an innate ability to evaluate and compare reality as it should be. As a rule, they have an internal set of rules, principles and standards, as if a person has swallowed a package of measuring instruments and always carries them with him, measuring and evaluating himself, other people and the world around him.

Inside, they have a strong critical voice with lots of "shoulds," reproaching both themselves and others. Therefore, they tend to do what is right from their critic's point of view, rather than what they really want to do. Units always think they know how it should be and how it should be done. Rules and structure are important to them.

"Let them comply with what was agreed. "
They behave quite reservedly, ready to take on work and family responsibilities. They are not interested in fashion trends or empty talk. They have a firm voice and a pronounced chin. They focus on the gray hair and not the rest of the black hair.

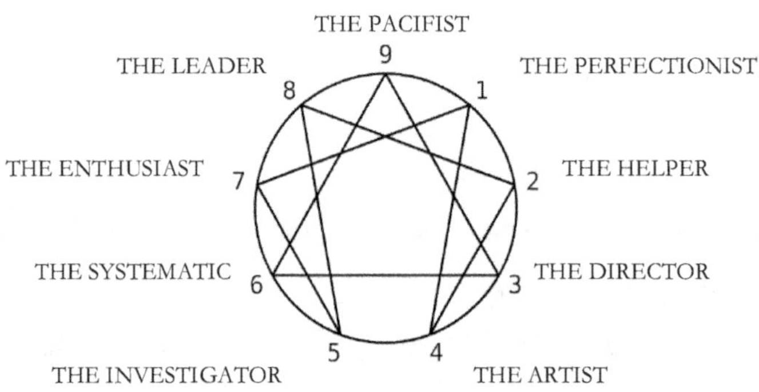

Constantly moving towards perfection, they rarely come into contact with their true feelings, and most often show anger or hatred, which is then expressed as irritation, resentment and guilt. They tend to delay things for fear of making mistakes; They find it difficult to take risks because of their need to be perfect. The main thing is to avoid "imperfection" at all costs. They are perfect and neat housewives. On many occasions they are more papist than the Pope.

Perfectionists are able to trace clear paths to resolve complex and uncertain situations and arrive at sober and objective evaluations. More than other Enneagram styles, Type 1s can be insightful,

dispassionate, and fair. While they adapt to the given environment, they tend to be overly understanding and passive. They withdraw from what they are feeling to avoid conflict.

CHARACTERS FROM SERIES AND MOVIES

In the series "Outlander", Claire Fraser is portrayed as a Type 1W2.

Photo taken from Netflix.

Claire gets into trouble because she can't ignore the inhuman values that surround her. She does not turn a "blind eye" to unfair situations, although they do not affect her directly. Claire is authentic, practical and capable. In fact, she gets her hands dirty and does things on her own. She feels the need to plan ahead and think through the circumstances instead of jumping in headfirst.

"I don't feel good about this. It is conceived as

unnecessarily risky as if we had not thought about it enough."

Her wing 2, being a doctor, allows her to help and heal people and be socially active. She is also aware of risk, danger and looks for things that last. She abandons Jamie and returns to Frank in the modern era. In order to maintain a relationship that does not satisfy them both, she does so out of obligation to her daughter, and only returns to Jamie once Brianna is older and Frank is dead.

She guides men and can step in front of them without hesitating to force her point of view. Leads plans in detail, although sometimes they are not successful. She is stubborn.

> "Even knowing that St. Germaine tried to poison me, I found it difficult to sentence him to death in cold blood."

This is where she pretends to see a shadow behind him as if it has special powers. Even though he has just admitted to poisoning her and being the head of the gang group that violently raped her young virgin friend in front of her eyes, she still finds pity in this man. After this, she is somehow able to impress the King of France and have him fall right into the palm of her hand. She proceeded to give both men at trial a poison that would sicken them, but not kill them in the hopes that the king would free them both."

She always tells Jamie and the others not to rush and then warns them of the results that could follow their lack of preparation due to their current feelings of anger and hatred. She fills her silence and knows when, where and how to compliment others to get what she wants. She never shows her feelings to others and even cheats on Jamie.

She chose not to rip Randall's balls off just so she could save her future husband's life. She remained calm in front of everyone when Randall showed up and was supposed to be dead or living in Scotland.

When French women murmur about a couple nibbling each other's ears behind a fireplace, she gets fed up and says, "Aren't any of you distressed by how the city treats its poor underprivileged people? I mean, surely you must see a staggering amount of them while traveling around the city. Just yesterday I saw a woman and her son dead in the middle of the road. It was horrible." Surely, we must do something to change the situation. The group of women seemed horrified and their response to the situation was to "remove those people to a less desirable part of town."

She gets angry and leaves the room and goes to the hospital to push herself too hard because she feels like she's not doing enough for the city. She thinks she needs to do several people's jobs because if she doesn't, who will? She doesn't even realize that she is unwell until the nursing nun orders her to rest. The only times she is compulsive is when it comes to justice in extreme situations (for example, someone being unfairly punished).

In the series "Friends", Monica Geller is portrayed as a Type 1W2.

Monica cares what people think and they want to keep up with appearances. She wants to be an important part of the community, which makes her strive to be valuable to others. This makes her even more of a perfectionist as she wants to be impressive. She works hard and wants others to recognize it, and this includes her loved ones.

"Excuse me for living in the real world!".

She always prioritizes the need to be productive over the need for social harmony. She is organized, rigid, desirous of order both in herself and in her environment, and motivated by good. When she thinks about herself, it's not about winning or getting ahead, but about her desire to be clean, organized, and extremely decisive.

"Welcome to the real world, it sucks, I'm going to love it".

She is very competitive, she did everything she could to pursue

her dream of being a chef and she became a very rational and logical person.

In the series "La Casa de Papel", The Professor is portrayed as a Type 1W9.

Photo taken from Netflix.

This character is in charge of plotting the entire plot, capturing the robbers and organizing a plan measured to perfection.

"There are people who study for years to earn a shitty salary, we are only going to study for five months".

He is intelligent, but also extremely calculating and obsessive. Something that, however, does not make him rush at any time, but rather allows him to occupy the role of patient observer.

Other famous quotes from the Professor:

"I already live with your mother, so marrying you doesn't

seem like that much of a problem to me either".

"We are going to carry out a plan that would be called crazy by anyone in their right mind. So, forget your senses".

"They have taught you in life to differentiate between good and bad. However, what we are doing has also been done by both people and banks, and nothing has happened."

The only exception he makes is with Inspector Raquel Murillo, with whom he falls madly in love without having anticipated it. This is something that destabilizes him and he makes mistakes. His personality fits with Enneagram One.

In the series "Game of Thrones", Daenerys Targaryen is portrayed as a Type 1W2.

Foto tomada de HBO

"The next time you raise your hand to me, it will be the last time you hold it. "
Shy and quiet, Daenerys Targaryen has grown stronger since becoming the wife of Dothraki chief Khal Drogo. This is what she told her brother Viserys. It is a phrase that makes you feel tremendous strength and never back down from fear.

"All men must die, but we are not men."

Daenerys said that expression when she was building a monument that symbolized power. Daenerys has a dragon and still has everything she wants. No one can bother her, even inevitable death. It's a line that talks about the success and strength of women in the real world.

"Dragons are not slaves."

This is what Daenerys said when her dragon didn't listen to the slaver enemy. If you tie up any person or animal, it will eventually leave you. If you want him to be on your side, you have to be considerate. This means that you should not force it down.

"I am the daughter of the dragon; I swear that anyone who tries to harm you will die screaming."

The dialogue has never been so bad (especially when you've made it out of the burning inferno unscathed).

In the series "Game of Thrones", Eddark (Ned) Stark is portrayed as a Type 1W9

"The man who pronounced the sentence must brandish the sword."

This sentence is full of Eddard's values. As a representative of Type 1W9, he thinks that leaders should never give orders or decisions that they cannot make for themselves. This can also be applied to our lives. It means that you shouldn't force people to do what you can't do.

"I learned to die a long time ago."

Ned Stark uttered this phrase to Varys, when he was trapped in a dungeon just before his death, which has an exciting and painful feeling. It is an expression that means that Eddard, who grew up as a warrior, has something more important than his own life.

The short answer is that he is ready to die at any moment. It's a line only Eddard can say as a perfectionist. He preaches that it is necessary to live without regrets as much as possible because we are in a situation where we can die today or in the next moment.

In the movie "The Gladiator", Maximus Decimus

Meridius is portrayed as a 1W2.

Photo taken from Netflix.

Maximus invokes guidance from his ancestors during his prayers, with his focus primarily on the past. He values the simple things in life, caring little for Marcus's grand ambitions or the pursuit of glory and authority. He dutifully and submissively follows the divine authority of the gods. His refusal to support Commodus stems from his disapproval of the emperor's assassination. Initially, Maximus avoids participating in gladiator combat as he fails to see its purpose. However, after connecting with Lucilla's son and recognizing her desire to protect him, he finds the motivation to challenge the emperor.

Maximus's actions are primarily driven by reactions. He initially fought for Marcus Aurelius' vision of Rome, and upon Aurelius' death, his motivation waned. It rekindled only when his family faced danger, shifting his purpose to seeking revenge.

Before Aurelius' passing, Maximus never fought for his personal convictions or vision. Even if he didn't desire the command, the anticipation of what was to come, the necessity to align Rome with the envisioned path, and the commitment to the greater good would have overridden his personal desires. He lacked foresight in recognizing the full extent of Commodus' true nature, similar to Quintus. It took Lucilla's persuasion to make him see that he could defeat Commodus, as he was unable to look past his current status as a slave. When Proximo urged him to win over the crowd, he did not consider it a significant or viable path.

In the "Naruto" series, Itachi Uchiha is portrayed as a 1W9

Photo taken from Netflix.

Itachi aims to encourage Sasuke to overcome his fear of the unknown and approach the future with courage and an open mind, emphasizing that fearing the unseen is foolish:

"It is foolish to fear what we have yet to see and know."

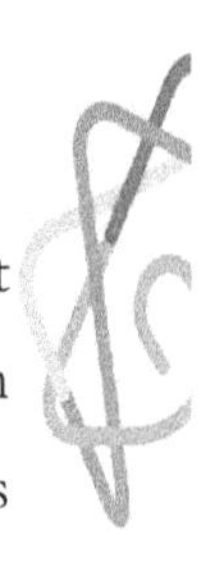

Itachi is a highly skilled and strategic ninja who excels at identifying his opponents' weaknesses. He imparts wisdom through quotes, such as, "Even the strongest of opponents always has a weakness," emphasizing the importance of recognizing vulnerabilities.

He highlights the significance of self-awareness and personal growth with statements like, "Those who cannot recognize themselves will eventually fail."

As a perfectionist, Itachi continually assesses his perspectives to evolve as an individual, acknowledging that knowledge and consciousness can be elusive.

"Knowledge and consciousness are vague, and perhaps better called illusions."

Itachi, who is considered one of the wisest in anime, advises Naruto who is willing to go to several places at once during the Fourth Great Ninja War. Being a perfectionist, Itachi advocates for seeking help and not bearing burdens alone, even as one becomes stronger, with the belief that failure is certain otherwise:

"No matter how strong you become, never try to endure everything alone. If you do, failure is certain."

He critiques his brother, Sasuke, for fixating on revenge,

emphasizing the importance of understanding and information to drive change. The "fog of ignorance" he refers to is a lack of clarity and understanding that prevents people from seeing the big picture and making educated judgments:

"Change is impossible in this fog of ignorance."

Itachi's code of honor prioritizes loyalty and honesty within a team, warning against turning against comrades, as such actions lead to dire consequences:

"Those who turn their heads against their comrades will surely suffer a terrible death."

Itachi's character embodies a knowledgeable hero veiled as a complex villain, driven by a pursuit of self-improvement.

ANALYSIS OF A BIBLICAL CHARACTER:

King David was born in Bethlehem; his father's name was Jesse. It is known that David had a pleasant appearance, a blond boy, being the youngest son of the family that tended sheep. When the prophet Samuel saw David for the first time, the voice of God appeared to him with the words: "Arise, anoint him, for he is it." It was about anointing for the kingdom. Samuel took the horn to anoint David's forehead with the words: "The Lord will be with you in all your works." This prophecy came true.

The following Bible passage in Psalms 78:70 shows him as a moral hero, typical of Type 1:

"He chose David also his servant, and took him from the sheepfolds".

At the court of the first Israeli king, Saul, the wonderful young man had the opportunity to become a musician and squire; David skillfully played the harp. King Saul was far from weak. The Scriptures describe him as tall and broad-shouldered, but not yet superior in strength to the Philistine Goliath. During one of the battles, Goliath asked a warrior to be his opponent and if he won, he promised that the Philistines would become slaves, but if the warrior lost to him, the Israelites would have to become slaves. Everyone was scared by these words, but David heard this and expressed his desire to fight the giant Goliath.

Everyone was amazed and bewildered: young David had not yet studied the art of war. But the words "The Lord will be with you in all your affairs" were not spoken in vain. As a shepherd, David even defeated lions and bears that invaded his flock.

David faced Goliath even without a helmet or armor because they seemed too heavy to him. Running towards Goliath, he threw a stone at him with his sling, pulled the giant's sword from its sheath, and cut off his head. The Philistines fled in terror. The people of Israel were saved.

Type 1s work hard. In this Bible passage in 2 Samuel 3:1 we can observe:

> "Now there was long war between the house of Saul and the house of David: but David waxed stronger and stronger, and the house of Saul waxed weaker and weaker".

When Saul and his heir Ishbosheth died, the elders of Israel came to Hebron, made a covenant with David, and anointed him king over all Israel (2 Sam. 5:3). The time of David's kingdom has arrived. David "reigned over Judah seven years and six months, and reigned in Jerusalem thirty-three years over all Israel and Judah" (2 Kings 5:5).

Type 1s are rarely satisfied with themselves. Let's look at the following Bible passage in 2 Samuel 23:13-17:

> "And three of the thirty chiefs went down, and came to David in the harvest time unto the cave of Adullam: and the troop of the Philistines pitched in the valley of Rephaim. And David was then in a hold, and the garrison of the Philistines was then in Bethlehem. And David longed, and said, oh that one would give me drink of the water of the well of Bethlehem, which is by the gate!
>
> And the three mighty men brake through the host of the

Philistines, and drew water out of the well of Bethlehem, that was by the gate, and took it, and brought it to David: nevertheless, he would not drink thereof, but poured it out unto the Lord. And he said, be it far from me, O Lord, that I should do this: is not this the blood of the men that went in jeopardy of their lives? therefore he would not drink it. These things did these three mighty men."

David was a wise and just ruler. The above is confirmed by the passage in the Bible in 2 Samuel 8:15:

"And David reigned over all Israel; and David executed judgment and justice unto all his people."

His love for the beautiful Bathsheba forced him to commit the sin of sending her husband Uriah to certain death. David repented of his sin before the Lord, who was angry with the king. The first son of David and Bathsheba died. But the Lord is merciful and David was forgiven. David and Bathsheba had a second son, Solomon, to whom David transferred his entire kingdom. The Lord loved Solomon.

Type 1 has high standards and principles. We can see it in the following Bible passage in 1 Kings 8:16:

"Since the day that I brought forth my people Israel out

of Egypt, I chose no city out of all the tribes of Israel to build a house, that my name might be therein; but I chose David to be over my people Israel. "

One of David's most notable phrases is: "The Lord is my shepherd; I shall not want." This powerful statement reminds us that, with faith and trust in God, we can overcome any obstacle that comes our way to success.

Type 1s always leave a legacy, which we can read in the following Bible passage in Mark 2:23-28:

"And it came to pass, that he went through the corn fields on the sabbath day; and his disciples began, as they went, to pluck the ears of corn. And the Pharisees said unto him, Behold, why do they on the sabbath day that which is not lawful? And he said unto them, have ye never read what David did, when he had need, and was an hungred, he, and they that were with him?

How he went into the house of God in the days of Abiathar the high priest, and did eat the shewbread, which is not lawful to eat but for the priests, and gave also to them which were with him? And he said unto them, the sabbath was made for man, and not man for the sabbath: Therefore, the Son of man is Lord also of the sabbath."

Try it for yourself

Maybe you belong to this Type 1, if you recognize the following:

☐ Do you often think about how to improve something?

☐ Do you try to avoid mistakes and bad actions?

☐ Do you have high moral standards?

☐ Do you value practical virtues: work, honesty, competence?

☐ Do you have an extremely strict inner critic that tells you what is right and what is wrong?

☐ Does your Inner Critic judge and control your emotions and needs?

☐ Do you sometimes feel resentful when others get their way too easily?

☐ Do you instinctively know how things could ideally be?

Healthy Mode

Healthy type ones are selfless and highly moral people. If they have a mission or a big task, they will work to achieve it with unwavering discipline and great courage. People of this type put ethics and personal integrity before any gain, income or easy decision. A type one might express himself like this: "I'm not here to do a job, make money, and die. I have to leave something behind. So that at the end of my life I can look back and realize that it all made sense."

Therefore, type ones, in a healthy mode, behave very consciously and do everything possible for the sake of high ideals. However, they are also able to forgive themselves and other people for mistakes, recognizing the fact that we are all learning and are at different stages of working on ourselves. They are able to accept the world as it is, without trying to fix or remake it. And, paradoxically, accepting this imperfection becomes the foundation for Type 1s to truly empathize and reform for the better.

Passion Capital

The passion capital for Type 1 is wrath, stemming from a dissatisfaction with the world's imperfections.

Integration and Disintegration

As a curious fact, if we divide the number 1 by 7 the result will be 0.142857142857, that is, the sequence of numbers that is reflected in the figure starting from enneatype 1 and ending at 7. That is the order of the direction disintegration: 1-4-2-8-5-7-1 plus the other line 9-6-3-9.

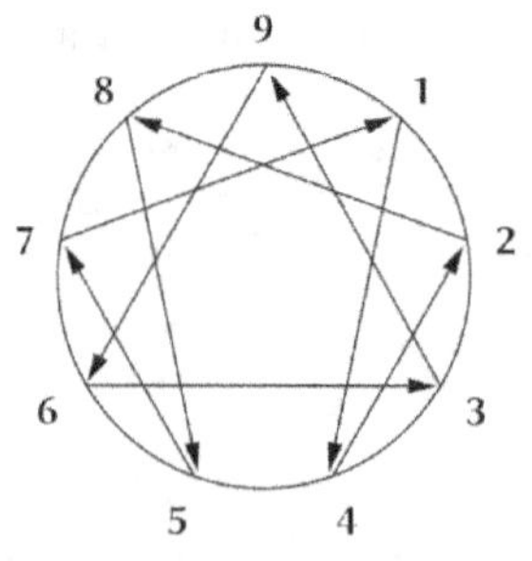

State of Stress, Unhealthy Mode or Disintegration from 1 to 4

When a perfectionist is under pressure and becomes insecure, he may recognize type four patterns in himself. He easily loses self-esteem and feels that his problems overshadow everything.

He accesses his emotions and thinks every time what didn't work well. At the same time, he becomes aware of other people's emotions, and how they perceive his behavior. He becomes lazy and lethargic in everything, disconnects from all problems and conflicts, does not deal with problems and becomes negligent.

Security or Integration from 1 to 7

When the Perfectionist is resourceful and feels secure, he or she uses type seven behavior patterns. You have lots of ideas, enjoy planning upcoming events, and dream about what you would like to do in the future. You are freed from the need to bring everything to perfection and it becomes easier for you to accept everything as it is, without correcting anything.

He accepts situations deeply, is emotionally stable and calm without appearing cold. Use empathy as a weapon to unite groups in harmony.

Development and growth path for Type 1

Recognize your emotions and impulses and realize that negative emotions quickly disappear when you accept them. In this way, you can free yourself from the desire to judge everyone and instead experience peace and clarity, leading you to a state of authentic existence, in which everything is perceived as perfect and subject to a higher "order."

Make an effort to fully enjoy and release repressed emotions, including feelings of anger. Look on the bright side of things, find a variety of pleasures and share them with others. For personal growth, Type 1s should recognize and accept their emotions, release repressed feelings, focus on positive aspects, and shift from "should" to "want."

Vice

Anger is experienced as indignation, driven by dissatisfaction. It can range from mild annoyance to hysterical rage and pure hatred.

 **How to communicate with a Type 1 person**

- When asking for a task, clarify the purpose, goals, and procedures. Additionally, it is better to clarify the role (scope of responsibility).

- If there is a change in what was decided, clearly communicate the reason.

- If you don't respond to comments, Type 1 is worried that he's wrong, so respond to him. Also, if you make a mistake, you have to admit it honestly because Type 1 is also worried about the other person's mistakes.

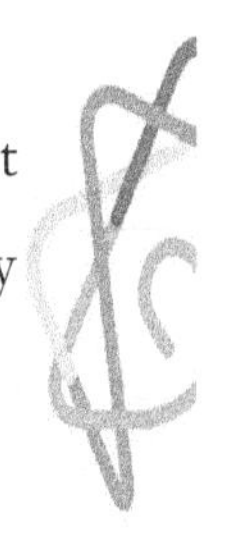

- If Type 1 people are diligent and hardworking, but are not appreciated by others, they become frustrated and very irritable, so listen to them carefully and respectfully.

Fixation

The fixation for Type 1 is condemnation, expressed through internal criticism or comments about others and upcoming events.

Virtue

The virtue of Type 1 is calmness, the ability to find contentment and inner peace.

Ethical integrity

Ethical integrity is a priority for Type 1, with respect being a key value.

Parameter intelligence

Type 1 individuals are related to the intelligence of parameters, which involves setting boundaries in time, space, action, or thought. Rigid parameters can lead to perfectionism and inflexibility, while the right direction allows for the establishment of new parameters.

Body expression

In terms of body expression, Type 1 often conceals dissatisfaction and anger by clenching their teeth, resulting in facial tension and a telling tone of voice.

Keywords that symbolize Type 1

Keywords that symbolize Type 1 include ideal, perfection, correctness, rigor, time, control, justice, honor student, criticism, notable flaws, frustration, diligence, and improvement.

THE HELPER

Eneatype 2 Server-Assistant

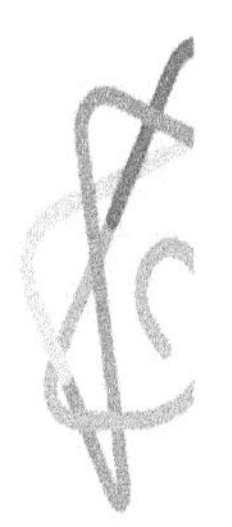

"Empathy arises when you feel another person's pain. But giving to others and not counting the cost is true empathy. Helping a suffering person is a drop in the ocean. However, without all these drops, the ocean would not would be complete."

Anonymous

 People and relationships hold significant importance for Type Twos. They are characterized by generosity, sociability, attentiveness, emotional warmth, love, dependence, responsibility, possessiveness, and at times, manipulative tendencies. Type Twos have a unique ability to see the best in others, often excelling in offering compliments and seeking validation in return. They can exhibit seductive, charming, and encouraging behaviors, with a strong inclination to please those around them.

The most remarkable gift of a Type Two lies in their capacity to cultivate deep, personal connections with people, appreciating them for who they are beyond mere appearances and behaviors. They often create an atmosphere of inclusivity, making everyone feel like a part of one big family.

Helpers possess an innate desire to give from the heart, but they frequently struggle with receiving in return. Type Twos tend to become more attuned to their own needs when they are alone and independent, as they often prioritize the wants and needs of others while neglecting their own. This imbalance can lead to somatic illnesses and conflicts within their relationships, sometimes manifesting as emotional outbursts or hysteria. Type Twos are also known for their pride and a sense of being indispensable:

"I do everything." "It's thanks to me that all of this exists, but no one cares about me."

Type Twos constantly seek the approval of others, which provides them with a sense of self-esteem and survival. Their focus on others' needs often takes the form of manipulation and control. They believe they know what's best for those around them and frequently aim to merge with others without conscious choice, all in the hope of gaining approval and love. This can sometimes lead to a blurring of boundaries between themselves and other individuals. Type Twos are generally seen as very open individuals with high emotional intelligence, ready to provide support in any situation.

They have a strong desire to be needed by people and often intrude in others' lives due to their excessive generosity. Despite giving a lot, they always expect something in return.

.

"Gratitude is all I want."

She's a well-behaved girl, yet she can transform into a captivating woman. She entices with absolute naiveté.

"I'm aware of my wonder, but I don't do it intentionally."

 Take a different perspective with diverse terms:

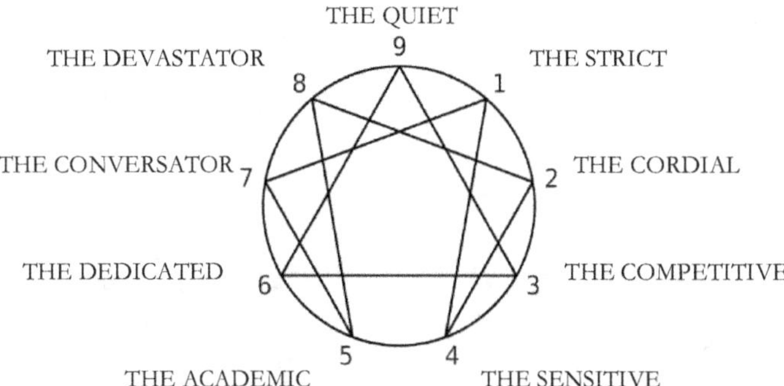

 **CHARACTERS FROM SERIES AND MOVIES**

In the series "Grey´s Anatomy", Isabel "Izzie" Stevens is portrayed as a Type 2W1.

Izzie displays her inability to maintain proper emotional distance from her patients, which results in her falling in love with one of them. Donate millions of dollars to save a patient's life. Her generosity and kindness is very indicative of a person committed to those around her, willing to offer everything she can.

Izzie displays an inability to maintain the appropriate emotional distance with her patients, resulting in her falling in love with one of them. She donates millions of dollars to save a patient's life. Her generosity and kindness are clear indicators of someone deeply committed to those around her, willing to give all she can.

She values her home more than her work, a recurring theme throughout the series. This not only jeopardizes her medical career but also her moral compass. She manages to create a home for those around her and enjoys shared holidays and moments. Even in her worst moments, she keeps everything running, albeit sometimes misinterpreting Alex's motives, succumbing to her relationship with George, and blaming Danny for the entire fiasco.

In the "The Walking Dead" series, King Ezekiel is portrayed as 2W3.

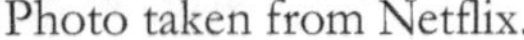

Photo taken from Netflix.

Ezequiel naturally makes decisions based on his emotions. He is generous, empathetic and humble. Your friends and family are the key focus of your life. King Ezekiel is forgiving and sincere, always looking for the good in others.

In the "Naruto" series, Sakura Haruno is portrayed as a 2W1

Sakura is sensitive to the feelings of others. The atmosphere in which she finds herself, she uses to evaluate situations and thus see how the circumstances match her values and beliefs, in order to act accordingly. Sakura, in the first seasons, was willing to leave the village with Sasuke.

When Naruto returns to the village, she realizes how much Sakura cares about him and the village, and not just Sasuke. She has a keen sense of her past experiences and uses them as motivation to continue progressing in the present.

She often places herself lower than her group, trying to work on the emotional atmosphere. She asks Tsunade for a teaching to help Naruto bring Sasuke home, not for clearly personal reasons. Additionally, she represses her negative emotions.

ANALYSIS OF A BIBLICAL CHARACTER:

A remarkable example of a biblical character who embodies the traits of Type 2 is Ruth.

Ruth: A Model of Compassion and Assistance

Ruth is a short but powerful book in the Old Testament of the Bible that recounts the story of a Moabite woman who, after becoming a widow, decides to stay with her Jewish mother-in-law, Naomi. Ruth is an extraordinary example of generosity, loyalty, and sacrifice, qualities that are fundamental to Type 2 in the Enneagram.

One of the key verses that demonstrates Ruth's altruistic nature can be found in Ruth 1:16-17 (King James Version): "And Ruth said, Intreat me not to leave thee, or to return from following after thee: for whither thou goest, I will go; and where thou lodgest, I will lodge: thy people shall be my people, and thy God my God: Where thou diest, will I die, and there will I be buried: the Lord do so to me, and more also, if ought but death part thee and me."

In these verses, Ruth expresses her unwavering commitment to her mother-in-law, Naomi. Despite the difficulties and challenges she will face in accompanying Naomi back to the land of Judah, Ruth is willing to sacrifice her own comfort and security for Naomi's well-being. This act of devotion and sacrifice clearly reflects the characteristics of Type 2 in the Enneagram, often described as "The Helper" due to their strong desire to be there for others, even at the expense of their own needs.

The Act of Harvesting to Sustain Naomi

One of the most prominent ways in which Ruth demonstrates her Type 2 nature is through her work in the fields, gleaning for grain to sustain both herself and Naomi. Ruth 2:2 (King James Version) presents this scene: "And Ruth the Moabitess said unto Naomi, let me now go to the field, and glean ears of corn after him in whose sight I shall find grace. And she said unto her, Go, my daughter."

Ruth, despite being a foreigner in the land of Judah, shows unwavering determination to help care for Naomi. Her willingness to toil tirelessly in the fields and gather grain reflects her desire to contribute and care for those she loves. This type of sacrifice for the well-being of others is a hallmark of Type 2 in the Enneagram.

The Encounter with Boaz: An Example of Connection and Assistance

Ruth eventually encounters Boaz, a close relative of Naomi, while gleaning in his fields. The relationship she develops with Boaz also illustrates the qualities of a Type 2 in the Enneagram. Boaz, upon learning of Ruth's loyalty and care for Naomi, shows his appreciation and gratitude toward her. Ruth 2:11-12 (King James Version) records this encounter: "And Boaz answered and said unto her, It hath fully been shewed me, all that thou hast done unto thy mother in law since the death of thine husband: and how thou hast left thy father and thy mother, and the land of thy nativity, and art come unto a people which thou knewest not heretofore. The Lord recompense thy work, and a full reward be given thee of the Lord God of Israel, under whose wings thou art come to trust."

In this passage, we see how Ruth receives recognition and gratitude from Boaz for her selfless actions in caring for Naomi. Type 2 individuals in the Enneagram often seek approval and emotional connection through their service to others, and Ruth experiences this when Boaz praises her dedication.

The Act of Selflessness and Commitment to Boaz

One of the most striking features of Ruth as a Type 2 in the Enneagram is her act of selflessness and commitment to Boaz, as found in Ruth 3:9 (King James Version): "And he said, Who art thou? And she answered, I am Ruth thine handmaid: spread therefore thy skirt over thine handmaid; for thou art a near kinsman."

In this pivotal moment in the story, Ruth approaches Boaz in the darkness and asks him to spread the corner of his garment over her, which is a symbolic gesture of a marriage proposal in the culture of that time. This act reflects the deep emotional connection and desire to care for and be cared for that characterizes Type 2. Ruth is willing to take the initiative to secure her own and Naomi's future, demonstrating her commitment and focus on the well-being of those she loves.

Ruth is an extraordinary example of a Type 2 in the Enneagram due to her altruistic nature, her desire to care for others, her

willingness to sacrifice her own needs, and her pursuit of emotional connection through service and assistance. Her story in the Bible offers a clear example of how Type 2 individuals can be compassionate and selfless figures who play a significant role in the lives of those around them. Ruth embodies the spirit of Type 2 in the Enneagram through her love and service to Naomi, Boaz, and her community as a whole.

Try it for yourself

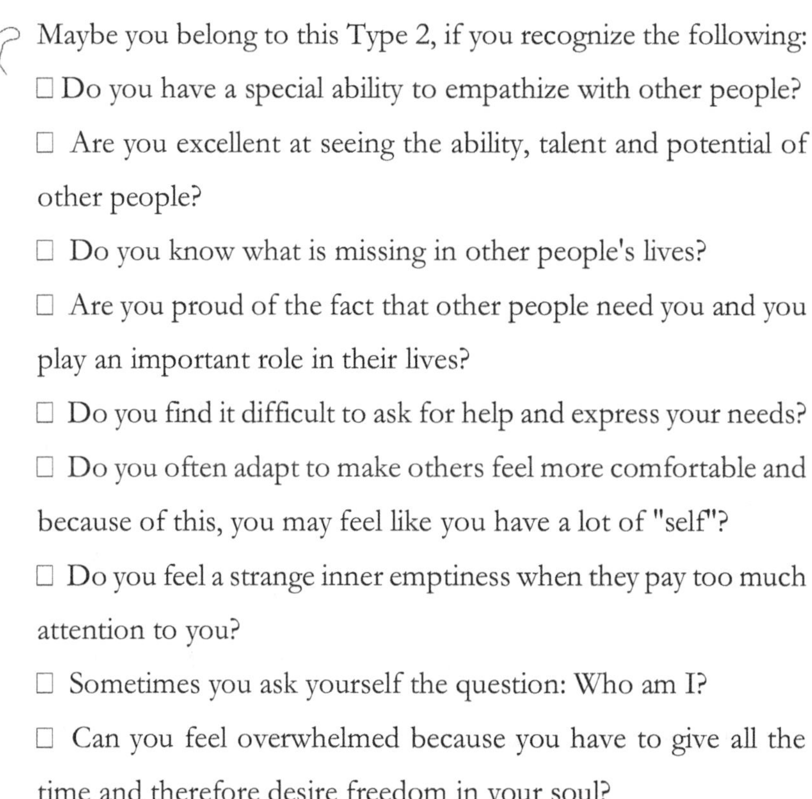

Maybe you belong to this Type 2, if you recognize the following:

☐ Do you have a special ability to empathize with other people?

☐ Are you excellent at seeing the ability, talent and potential of other people?

☐ Do you know what is missing in other people's lives?

☐ Are you proud of the fact that other people need you and you play an important role in their lives?

☐ Do you find it difficult to ask for help and express your needs?

☐ Do you often adapt to make others feel more comfortable and because of this, you may feel like you have a lot of "self"?

☐ Do you feel a strange inner emptiness when they pay too much attention to you?

☐ Sometimes you ask yourself the question: Who am I?

☐ Can you feel overwhelmed becuase you have to give all the time and therefore desire freedom in your soul?

Healthy Mode

Healthy Type 2s perceive all people as their brothers and sisters, and consider caring for them as the deepest meaning of their being. They also understand that when they do something good for another person, they are enriched by it. They like to give simply for the sake of the process itself. And someone else's joy becomes your joy. Therefore, healthy Type 2s do not expect anything in return for their love for people, since love itself is their greatest reward.

They easily sense other people's wants and needs. And they can freely help others without changing their minds and without forgetting, first of all, their needs. Whatever Type Two wants to share, he gives freely, because he himself has plenty.

The second commandment established by Jesus Christ "Love your neighbor as yourself" is also the essence of Type 2. Many have been known in the history of humanity to create societies and institutions to help those in need: the sick, children and the weak.

Passion Capital
Pride.

 **State of Stress, Unhealthy Mode or Disintegration from 2 to 8**

When Type Twos are under pressure and do not have enough self-confidence, they begin to display Type 8-character traits and more quickly descend into aggression. Suddenly, they are

absolutely aware of what they need, what they want, and they begin to control the situation with a style that surprises their loved ones. Justice becomes important to the Helper, and they may feel that others do not respect them. Instills guilt in others by manipulating them and making them feel indebted to them.

Security or Integration from 2 to 4

When the Helper feels safe, he begins to display Type 4 behavior patterns. He becomes more creative and aware of what is important to him. He begins to appreciate the intensity, sharpening the feelings. It becomes important for him to take an individual approach to business, to do everything on his own, in a special way, striving to show creativity and doing it with pleasure. This generates a loving, humble, selfless behavior with a vocation for service.

Development and growth path for Type 2

It's about recognizing your needs and desires. Learn to trust yourself to ask for and receive help from others. When a desire to please others arises, be aware of this desire and ask yourself the question: "Maybe this is my way of avoiding my own desires and needs? Or maybe this is my way of manipulating other people? You have to learn to say "no" consistently. Do what you feel comfortable doing for yourself.

Be kind to people without expecting anything in return. Don't tend to think that our desire is to fulfill the wishes of others, so you ask yourself what you really want.

Like a healthy Type 4, you can look inward, notice your abilities and charms; and build good relationships without depending on others by taking pride in yourself.

Vice

Pride is experienced as a feeling of satisfaction when Type Twos succeed and help other people.

 **How to communicate with a Type 2 person**

- Express recognition and gratitude for what a Type Two person does or contributes.

- At work, it is easier for people to demonstrate their abilities if they are placed in positions that are appreciated by people and where it is easy to see that they are useful.

- Type 2 people often do not express their opinions and thoughts in words.

- Take time to have a dialogue to elicit your thoughts.

- Intimacy-seeking Type 2s are very afraid of being rejected by others, so don't get emotionally angry when you make a point, but use a "thinking of you attitude."

Fixation

It is important for Type Twos to express and receive gratitude. A smile, a nod, or a verbal acknowledgment that someone said

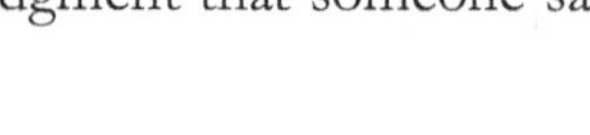

or did something good.

Virtue

Modesty is the understanding that this is not just my merit, but that I am just a part of something more.

Unconditional love relationships

Attention and Esteem.

Affective Intelligence

Type 2 are related to Affective Intelligence whose expression is the capacity to love, discerning and optimizing the various types of affectivities and integrating gratitude, compassion, humility or the commitment to unconditionality.

Keywords that symbolize Type 2

Likes and dislikes, good socialization, Warm, Affectionate, Sociable, Friendly, Egocentric, Desire for deep relationships, Appreciation, Affectionate, Obsessed, Service, Preserving one's own needs.

STATUS FINDER

Achiever-Star Enneatype
3

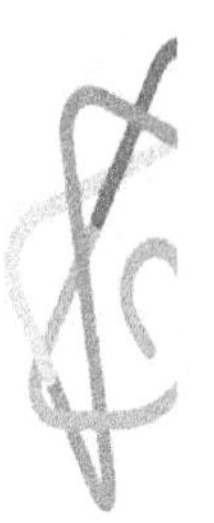

"Whatever my task is, I want to achieve it, solve it and move on. I don't want to be part of the problem; I want to be able to solve it. I don't want to get bogged down in that."

Anonymous

Achievers are always busy, goal-oriented. They are popular, successful, persuasive, assertive, competitive, positive, energetic, efficient, socially agile, narcissistic and hostile. They are excellent for planning for the future. The appearance of success is essential for type 3s, since they are very oriented to status and the image they create. They are fast-paced and like to be the center of attention.

Three is the most competitive and achievement-oriented Enneagram type. Unlike Type 2s, Type 3s are less concerned with ideas of helping other people and identify more with an image of success and productivity. Emotionally, they confuse the appearance of an accomplished person with being the "less than perfect" true self.

They have a tendency toward narcissism by constantly seeking to give a good image to others, making their appearance speak in their favor to cover their insecurities. Type Threes often keep themselves busy to keep any of their inappropriate feelings under control.

They feel loved more for what they do and do than for what they are and they hide what they really feel and think. At work, they make good decisions and strive to succeed. Their fear is of being insignificant or unfortunate.

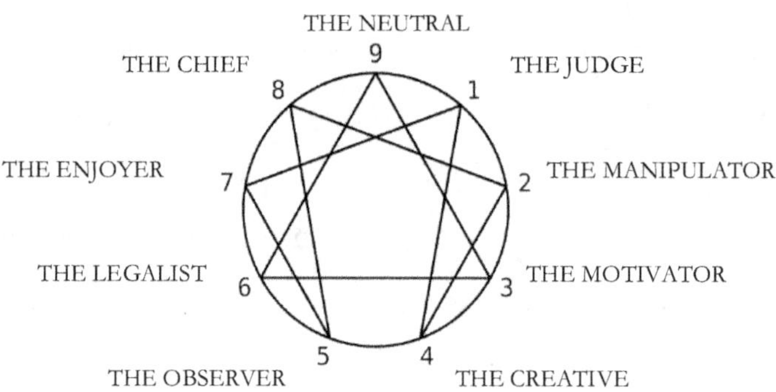

To avoid intimacy, they become workaholics and take on multiple projects at the same time, which in turn leads to a complete breakdown before realizing that they have been ignoring their needs. They are afraid of being rejected.

Work is extremely important to Type Threes, relationships are secondary, and true intimacy is difficult.

"Let them admire me."

The center of your mind is in the heart. Emotions and feelings are used to achieve your image. The main thing is to look good in the eyes of others, and therefore they rarely come into contact with their feelings, neglecting their inner world.

Salespeople in the marketing department

The Type 3 represents a personality driven by a burning desire for success, recognition, and accomplishments. These folks are all about chasing excellence and the need to stand out both in their personal and professional lives. They are incredibly ambitious, goal-oriented, and ready to hustle to reach their objectives.

One of the defining features of a Type 3 is their innate thirst for excelling and bagging accolades. This drive fuels their intense competitiveness and an unwavering commitment to delivering results. In the workplace, it translates to going above and beyond to achieve and surpass sales targets and earn recognition within their teams.

Type 3s also deeply care about their image and how others perceive them. They are very conscious of how they present themselves and often project an aura of success and confidence. This quality can be particularly valuable in the marketing arena since a brand's image and reputation are pivotal in attracting customers and gaining their trust.

However, it's important to note that Type 3 individuals may sometimes be so laser-focused on achieving results that they might neglect aspects of their personal lives and interpersonal relationships. They may constantly feel the pressure to maintain an image of perfection, which can occasionally lead to a lack of authenticity.

Their work ethic, competitive nature, and knack for projecting an image of success make them valuable assets in the marketing industry, where achieving results and managing a brand's image are paramount. Nonetheless, it's crucial for Type 3 individuals to strike a balance between professional success and a fulfilling personal life for overall well-being.

 **CHARACTERS FROM SERIES AND MOVIES:**

In the "The Simpsons" series, Charles Montgomery Burns is portrayed as a 3W4.

Mr. Burns is either a ruthless businessman stuck in the past, or a weak old grump, barely able to crush a paper cup. Come up with a plan to block the sun and make the city dependent on its power plant.

Mr. Burns makes very characteristic gestures and hand movements other than saying "excellent" and tapping his fingertips. He is a smart and lonely villain who seems to have a

master plan because he is very good at planning and there is a stereotype about that.

Martin Prince, appears to Mr. Burns with a model of a power plant and Mr. Burns responds with "It's too cold, where is the heart? " Mr. Burns sees a man on television (Frank Grimes) and relates to him enough to hire him as his vice president. Frank arrives at work and Mr. Burns sees a dog he loves so much on television, so he replaces Frank Grimes.

He is willing to spend his entire fortune on a teddy bear he had as a child and cries for the innocence of Maggie's childlike nature. He cares much more about the extravagant things he could do with his fortune than about maintaining it. He throws ideas everywhere and few of them are capable of existing in reality. Like when he opened his own casino.

Mr. Burns's embodiment of stereotypes about the image of corporate America is very similar to Type 3. For Mr. Burns, this image is an obsession with wealth and power, even going so far as to show a lack of concern for the safety of the employees.

This, combined with using his wealth on extravagant things, sounds a lot like an unhealthy Social Type 3. Beatrice Chestnut describes the Social Three in the following ways: "Its fuel is social success, although what exactly constitutes success can vary depending on the history and context of individual Social Threes.

Some show intelligence, culture or class; others have degrees and titles; and others have material symbols of social status: a nice house, an expensive car, designer clothes, or expensive watches. […] They are also focused on power, whether or not they are the ones who have it. They tend to be demanding and authoritarian, although these characteristics may be hidden behind a soft, decorous and humorous presentation.

Social Threes may view others in terms of how they can promote or block the process of achieving their goals. They look at things in terms of how they can exert control over them, and they do not allow themselves to be surprised by life. […] The Social Three is also the most aggressive of the Threes, it has a strong and assertive character. Because they are good at numbing your feelings, and can, in the extreme, be cold.

Social Type 3 has a corporate mindset and a passion for doing the job to the best of its ability, especially in terms of outward appearance. They think about what is best for the group, especially based on what will sell, what will look good, and what will reflect well on them." (Chestnut: 2013).

In the "Friends" series, Rachel Green is portrayed as a 3W4.

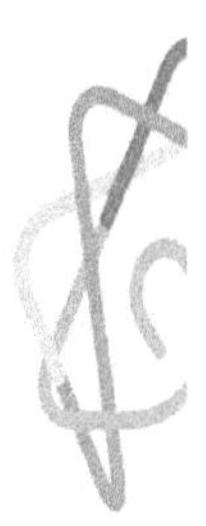

Photo taken from NBC.

Rachel throughout the series becomes much more emotionally secure and unafraid to be honest, while her logic excels at her job when she needs to think quickly. She is a healthy Type 3, always reacting to her surroundings and judging what she can see clearly.

Rachel doesn't behave childishly to appear cute and make others take care of her. Aspire to be independent and strong-willed. She is clearly very conscious of her image. She wants to appear like the typical beautiful popular woman. It expresses more vanity than pride. She is very prone to creating an image different from her true self, in order to make a more memorable impression and influence people.

The fact that he was embarrassed to go running with Phoebe because her running style was weird is very Type 3. Also, when that popular former classmate asked Monica out and Rachel pretended that he was interested in her. On another occasion, she pretended she was in love with a dumb blonde boy, whom she dated for a short time, to make Ross jealous. All of the above indicates the behavior of a Type 3w4.

She is individualistic, envious and focused on her career. Even when she appears lively and very talkative, it seems like nothing more than a facade. She is afraid of not reaching her full potential and that drives her to achieve her dreams of working in the fashion industry, and she does it all on her own. She is also motivated to sell an attractive and polished image to seduce those she is interested in.

Rachel is more comfortable living in the moment, and is even a bit reckless and impulsive, taking life as it comes. She spontaneously misses out on her wedding and moves in with Monica without taking much time to think about it. She decides at the last minute (after planning to stay in New York with a pregnant Phoebe) to fly to England to tell Ross that she loves him.

She is attuned to what is happening around her and can quickly and easily notice details in her surroundings, for example noticing Monica's new shoes. She feels more comfortable living in the moment and is annoyed when Ross begins to plan their future together. Rachel enjoys sensory pleasures, is very in tune with what is fashionable and has very glamorous taste, which is

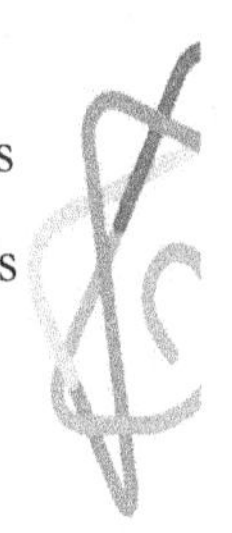

evident in the imaginary wedding she had dreamed of. Rachel is very sensitive to criticism and does not react well when she feels embarrassed.

She can tend to be quite selfish and is not very good at picking up on other people's feelings. She had no idea that Ross was in love with her until Chandler explicitly stated it. The reason Rachel and Ross clash so often, have so many arguments, and struggle to resolve their problems is because they both prioritize their own feelings and values over each other's and struggle to see things from the other's point of view.

There are many times where Rachel tries to push away her feelings in order to try to solve her problems using objective logic, but ultimately in the end she always follows her heart and cannot ignore her feelings (e.g., telling Ross who loves him even after making a deal with Monica, saying that Monica should make all the decisions for her). She once decided to follow Joey's advice to make a move on a guy simply because she liked him, showing her strong preference for feelings over reason.

Rachel is quite calm and in a group setting, she generally goes with the flow and lets others take a leadership role (usually Monica). And she is happy to follow her, but when something clashes with her feelings or values, she is very resistant, tough. She is willing and quick to fight back (for example, by yelling at Ross for planning her future for her or scolding Gunther for leaving work for personal reasons).

She often takes the time to figure out how she feels about things, such as Ross having a crush on her while in China, and realizing on the plane to Paris that she is in love with him and would rather be with him, than working for Louis Vuitton.

When faced with a problem, Rachel prefers to follow her heart, but will often try to push away her feelings to fix things using the most obvious solution (e.g., staying away from Ross because of Emily). She adapts to her new life quite easily and quickly learns to be efficient, resourceful and responsible.

When she feels strongly about something, she is quick to put those feelings into action; for example, leaving her job as a waitress to pursue a career in fashion, something she is very passionate about, and constantly works hard to move forward in her professional career. Rachel likes to talk to her friends while solving problems and asking them for their opinions and thoughts.

Rachel likes to feel like she is moving forward in her life and career. She breaks up with Tag because she wants to progress and feels like her love life is being held back due to her dating someone much younger and less mature than her.

In the "Grey's Anatomy" series, Cristina Yang is portrayed as a 3W4.

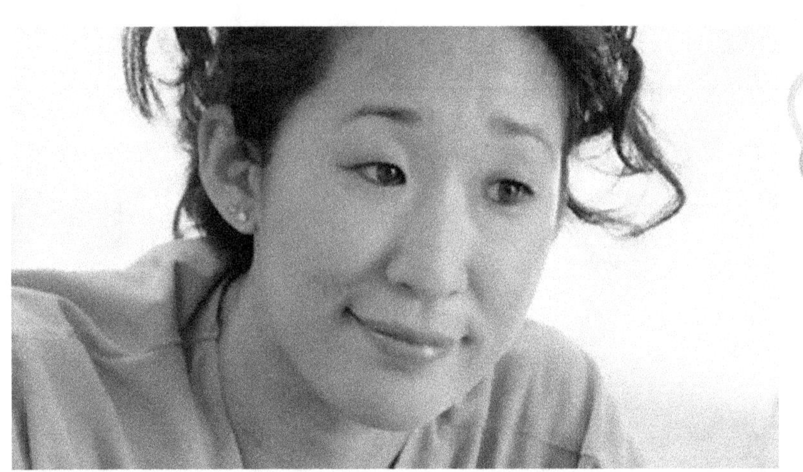

Photo taken from ABC Studios.

Much of the story is the work to climb the ladder by paying attention to external systems and using them as best as possible for the ability to climb that ladder. Cristina is intelligent and capable of progressing. She knows the system and knows how it works; Furthermore, she uses external situations to get ahead and doesn't pay as much attention to every little detail.

She is very progressive, goal-oriented and her thinking is directed toward meeting work and personal goals. Cristina is very detached from her feelings and other people, but she is not oblivious to them, as many believe.

The present moment and her surroundings are not a big concern for her, but her mind is incredibly organized, along with her work ethic. Cristina is extremely goal-oriented and high achiever. She puts her work before anything. For example, after suffering a miscarriage, her first priority was returning to work. Always tries to keep work and friends separate.

In the "Game of Thrones" series, Jamie Lannister is portrayed as a 3W2

Photo taken from ABC Studios.

"It is for love".

This was the phrase that Jamie Lannister said when pushing little Brandon from the tower because he saw him having relations with his sister, Queen Cersei. Don't we all have moments when we must do things, that we don't want to do, for love? It can be for family, friends or yourself.

In the "Yo soy, Betty la Fea" series, Patricia Fernández, "La Peliteñida" is portrayed as a 3W4.

Patricia seeks approval, like any enneagram 3, but she does not need to be loved and rewarded for what she does; Therefore, being an enneagram Type 3 with wing 4, unhealthy, she feels that just because she is her she is already special, and places her

feelings above those of others for being her, (like the multiple times she influenced and manipulated Marcela to help her get out of her troubles with the sole reason of "I am your best friend, what will people think when they see a person so close to Marcela Valencia in x unfavorable situation? ").

She is dominant and uses her attractiveness and body to be admired and desired, and, along with the 4th wing, she also looks for a "savior," a person who solves all her problems (in this case financial) because she deserves it.

"I studied finance for six months at San Marino. "

It was a phrase that secretary Patricia Fernández, "La Peliteñida" always said to show off her level of preparation, in a university of little prestige, when someone wanted to question her.

In the "Naruto" series, Naruto Uzumaki is portrayed as a 3W2.

Foto tomada de Netflix

He makes decisions based on his emotions and highly values friendship with others and mutual support. Naruto likes to feel appreciated and recognition is key to his happiness. He is ambitious, charming and enthusiastic. Naruto is goal and objective oriented and is not afraid to take initiative. Naruto Uzumaki has achieved great things in the world, which is typical of Type 3s. With exceptional ability when it comes to reading people, Naruto Uzumaki naturally adapts to different social situations.

Naruto has many friendships, but none as complex and strong as his friendship with Sasuke. They grew up together and, while fighting often, eventually became best friends.

Over time, Sasuke caused a lot of pain to Naruto and his other friends, but despite everything, Naruto would never give up and would fight the villains more if necessary. While Sasuke was

proud, he also loved Naruto like a brother, and ended up showing how much he cares during battles:

> "I don't care who I have to fight! If he rips my arms off, I'll kick him to death! If he rips off my legs, I'll bite him off! If he takes my head off, I'll watch him to death! And if he puts out my eyes, I'll curse him from the grave! Even if I am torn to pieces, I will get Sasuke back from Orochimaru! "

Naruto is a goofy, naive, and optimistic character who has had to face some heartbreaking losses. And even if situations got difficult for Naruto or his loved ones, he always found his way back to his positive mindset.:

> "The pain of being alone is completely out of this world, isn't it? "I don't know why, but I understand your feelings so much that it actually hurts. "

Naruto is one of the hardest-working anime heroes of all time, a positive quality that fans admire about him. While he is not as talented, strong, or popular as Sasuke, he never gives up and always trains to strengthen his physical and mental condition.

No matter how hard his training is or if he seems unable to learn a complicated Jutsu, he never gives up. His fighting mentality helped him ultimately achieve his dreams by becoming a powerful and respected ninja:

"Do not underestimate me! I don't give up and I don't beg! You can act tough all you want! You're not going to scare me! No way! I don't care if I'm stuck as a Genin for the rest of my life! Someday I will be Hokage. "

"I never give up! I will become Hokage no matter what!"

"I'll show you that I'm not someone you can just ignore!"

ANALYSIS OF A BIBLICAL CHARACTER:

A biblical character who vividly embodies the traits of Type 3 is Joseph, the son of Jacob. Throughout his story in the Old Testament, Joseph impressively demonstrates the distinctive qualities of a Type 3.

Joseph and his Ambitious Dream

A fundamental aspect of Type 3 is the desire for success and recognition. From an early age, Joseph shows an innate desire to excel and achieve success. Genesis 37:5-7 (King James Version) recounts a pivotal moment in Joseph's life: "And Joseph dreamed a dream, and he told it his brethren: and they hated him yet the more. And he said unto them, Hear, I pray you, this dream which I have dreamed: For, behold, we were binding sheaves in the field, and, lo, my sheaf arose, and also stood upright; and, behold, your sheaves stood round about, and made obeisance to my sheaf."

In these verses, Joseph shares a dream in which he sees himself standing out among his brothers. His sheaf of wheat rises and stands upright, symbolizing his desire to stand out and be admired. This desire for success and recognition is characteristic of Type 3 in the Enneagram, often described as highly achievement-oriented individuals who strive to be the best at what they do.

Joseph's Ascension in Egypt

Joseph goes through numerous challenges and adversities in his life, but his ambition and determination lead to a meteoric rise in Egypt. He becomes a high-ranking official of Pharaoh and is entrusted with the management of the land of Egypt. Genesis 41:41-43 (King James Version) records his ascent: "And Pharaoh said unto Joseph, See, I have set thee over all the land of Egypt. And Pharaoh took off his ring from his hand, and put it upon Joseph's hand, and arrayed him in vestures of fine linen, and put a gold chain about his neck; And he made him to ride in the second chariot which he had; and they cried before him, Bow the knee: and he made him ruler over all the land of Egypt."

Joseph achieves exceptional success in Egypt, becoming a figure of authority and power. His ability to excel and stand out in his work reflects the characteristics of Type 3 in the Enneagram, often described as highly achievement-oriented individuals. Type 3s are known for setting ambitious goals and working tirelessly to achieve them, and Joseph epitomizes this approach.

The Quest for Approval and Recognition

One of the distinctive features of Type 3 in the Enneagram is the desire for approval and admiration. Joseph seeks approval both from his father and his brothers. Genesis 37:3-4 (King

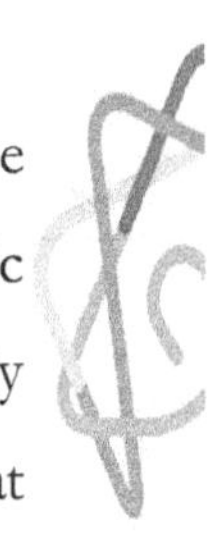

James Version) shows us this: "Now Israel loved Joseph more than all his children, because he was the son of his old age: and he made him a coat of many colours. And when his brethren saw that their father loved him more than all his brethren, they hated him, and could not speak peaceably unto him."

Joseph is praised and favored by his father, arousing envy and resentment among his brothers. His desire to be admired and stand out in the eyes of others is a fundamental characteristic of Type 3 in the Enneagram. Type 3 individuals often seek approval from authority figures and strive to maintain an image of success and achievement.

Joseph as an Example of Transformation

As Joseph's story progresses, he faces significant challenges and experiences profound personal growth. Despite his success in Egypt, Joseph also encounters moments of adversity and testing. His ability to adapt and learn from his experiences is a valuable quality that is also found in Type 3s in the Enneagram.

Joseph eventually forgives his brothers for their betrayal and shows compassion towards them, demonstrating a significant shift in his perspective. This act of forgiveness and compassion is an example of how Type 3s can transform and evolve throughout their lives.

Conclusion: Joseph, a Prominent Example of Type 3 in the Enneagram

In summary, Joseph, the son of Jacob, is a prominent example of Type 3 in the Enneagram due to his desire for success, his quest for approval and recognition, his ability to excel and stand

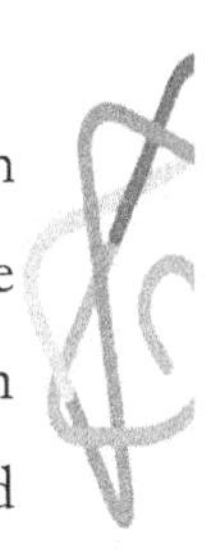

out in his work, and his willingness to adapt and transform throughout his life. His story in the Bible vividly illustrates the characteristics and challenges of a Type 3 and how determination and personal growth can lead to a life of accomplishment and significance. Joseph embodies the spirit of Type 3 in the Enneagram through his journey from envy and the pursuit of success to compassion and personal transformation.

Try it for yourself

Maybe you belong to this Type 3, if you recognize the following:

☐ Are the main things for you: efficiency, productivity, goals and results?

☐ Is it important for you to be successful and avoid failure?

☐ Do you put your soul into your work and identify with it: you are what you do?

☐ Is it easy for you to let go of your emotions and do you often not have enough time?

☐ Are you good at following the rules and playing the role required to achieve your goal?

☐ Is it difficult for you not to be active and rest, for example, during cleaning or repair?

☐ Are you good at focusing on a goal for a long time, as well as finding different approaches to achieve it?

☐ If necessary, you can change roles and image, it has the qualities of a "chameleon".

☐ Do you easily motivate other people and are you a great role model?

Healthy Mode

Healthy Type 3s are incredibly good at setting and achieving goals and typically develop many life skills. They sincerely strive for personal development and excellence in everything they do. They are organized, flexible and hardworking.

Representatives of the third type learn quickly and show themselves best in complex and highly social professions, where their performance is measured by specific results. Inspiring and inspired, all 3 are optimistic believers in their abilities, wholeheartedly and without irony.

Healthy Type 3s are energetic and fun, with a positive view of the future and self-confidence in solving problems. They become good role models and teachers of the skills they have developed in themselves, that is, they are a model of what they themselves talk about. And they have a good sense of humor about themselves and their behavior. They value their family and relationships as much as their work and are scrupulously honest. In general, type 3 reflects the best in the ability to act, and sometimes 3s show a unique ability to get things done efficiently and productively. They are especially good for multitasking. At the same time, they are neutral in the face of the difficulties that arise, not perceiving them too emotionally or close to their hearts.

Passion Capital

The Vanity.

State of Stress, Unhealthy Mode or Disintegration from 3 to 9

If the Type Three is under emotional pressure or exhaustion, then they display Type 9 behavior patterns. Suddenly it becomes difficult for them to prioritize, all tasks become equally important. Type Three has a hard time getting work done and seems to be going in circles and nothing is working. Lies or deceives others to obtain praise or evaluations from others due to extreme fear of failure.

Security or Integration from 3 to 6

When the Achiever is in a confident and resourceful state, he exhibits Type 6 behavior patterns. He realistically evaluates his tasks, taking into account the time and resources available to him. It is easy for you to analyze the consequences and take a healthy skeptical approach to the matter.

Efficient and highly capable, but seeking to succeed in a higher position leads to self-defense and exclusivity to look better than they really are, regardless of the means.

Development and growth path for Type 3

- You are completely honest with yourself and with others. The development of your Type 3 will be facilitated by slowing down to develop inner peace, awareness of accessing your emotions, and working on the belief that "I am loved no matter what I do, whether I succeed or not."

- Because you are trapped in the image of yourself that you can do it, you must pause the constant movement towards your goals and be free to explore your true feelings, which you usually ignore.

- Stay away from people's evaluations and achievements. Enjoy interacting with people outside of work, play a sport, or pursue hobbies.

- A sense of self-congruence comes from recognizing yourself "pretending" to look good to others and striving to convey what you really think.

- Through service and loyalty to those around you, you realize that being part of something larger than themselves does not change your worth and you discover true self-worth as a healthy Type Six.

Vice

Self-deception: occurs when the Achiever begins to play this or that role to obtain something significant. To do this, they "turn off" their emotions and focus on the objectives and the result.

 **How to communicate with a Type 3 person**

- If there are accomplishments or processes worth praising a Type 3, be willing to put them into words.

- Type 3 people have a good image of themselves, which is why it is difficult for them to accept complaints. So, when you want to point something out, first talk to them about what they have done and their good image. That

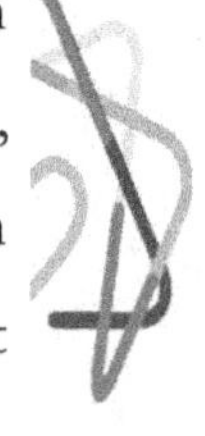

softens your claim.

- When Type 3 people have to deal with their emotions, help them face themselves by telling them that there are things more important than success.

- For Type 3s, vanity is experienced as the importance of status, image, and fashion. It is important for them to look good and make an excellent impression, both with their appearance and with their competition. Understand them.

Virtue

Honesty: the ability to be completely honest, to act based on true emotions.

Authenticity

Recognition and Estimation.

Motivational Intelligence

Those of Type 3 are related to Motivational Intelligence: It is the ability to motivate oneself and others. People with high motivational intelligence have a great ability to inspire and motivate others.

Keywords that symbolize Type 3

Efficient, hard-working, conceited, skilled, boastful, admirable, self-respect, achievement-oriented, success, status.

THE ARTIST

Individualist-Tragi-romantic Enneatype 4

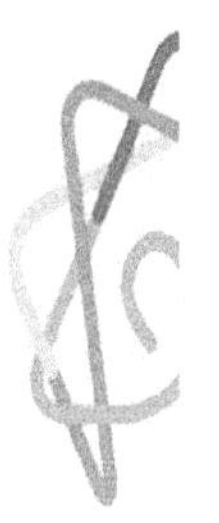

"I'm not sure anyone else is capable of perceiving events, places, or things with such an abundance of detail, richness, and breadth as Type 4s. Even if I'm bored, it's intense boredom."

Anonymous

Type Fours tend to be creative, romantic, introverted, artistic, bohemian, intuitive, melancholic, and depressive. They are emotional and dramatize their emotions by taking everything personally. Mood can change many times a day. In all manifestations of life, they seek beauty, they passionately desire to be loved.

In Type 4 people, the feeling of abandonment rules. They see themselves as part of a very special story, and their way of perceiving things tends to lead them to a strong emotional burden that turns them into tragic and melancholic people.

Their outward appearance is dramatic and they suffer from low self-esteem caused by the belief that they are not worth staying with. They have a fundamental need to be special, unique, they hate being ordinary. They are creative. Karl Abraham mentions a term of oral-aggressive behavior to the frustrated and complaining Type 4. (Abraham: 1965).

Type Fours are sensitive to other people's suffering and want to alleviate it. Helping people gives them drive, passion, and a sense of purpose. Type 4s can understand another person's stress and pain. At their best, 4s are a reflection of the inner world for all of us, also expressing and affirming the reality of inner life, insisting that dreams and emotions are as real as a chair and a table. They can be great teachers or therapists.

They are constantly exploring themselves and looking for different ways to deal with their emotions. And they tend to live vividly, experiencing strong feelings such as curiosity, the desire to live, passion and even anger. They are individualistic in nature and like to think of themselves as unique people differentiated from the rest.

Something tragic and unattainable or a physical risk gives them an acute experience of their emotions. The intense comparison of themselves with other people and the belief that others have what they lack, leads them into the trap of envy and makes them very competitive.

Melanie Klein mentions: "I came to the conclusion that envy is

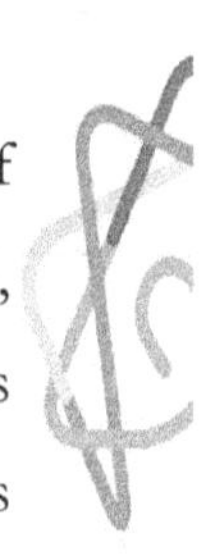

the most powerful factor in undermining the roots of feelings of love and gratitude, since it affects the earliest relationship of all, the maternal relationship. The fundamental importance of this relationship for the entire emotional life of the individual has been exposed in a whole series of psychoanalytic writings, and I believe that by having further explored a specific factor that can be very disturbing at this early age, I have added something important to my previous discoveries relating to child development and personality formation." (Klein: 1988).

They may be prone to suffering, depression, regret and self-criticism, sometimes with an internal feeling of resentment. They are worried about themselves and narcissism; dreams of exciting projects. Often, Type Fours are burdened with a distorted idea of their body, forcing them to achieve the "ideal" by any means. Sometimes this leads to anorexia or bulimia.

"Let them understand me."

Type 4 people love deep and intimate relationships, they do not communicate on a superficial level, they like to give a personal touch to what they do. They can be in tune with the group, but one on one is better; can help those who suffer and need it.

Type Fours can be good therapists, psychologists, and teachers because they have a sense of empathy. They are sensitive and show their emotions as they are. Extremely creative with emotional strength and sensitivity.

VIRTUES

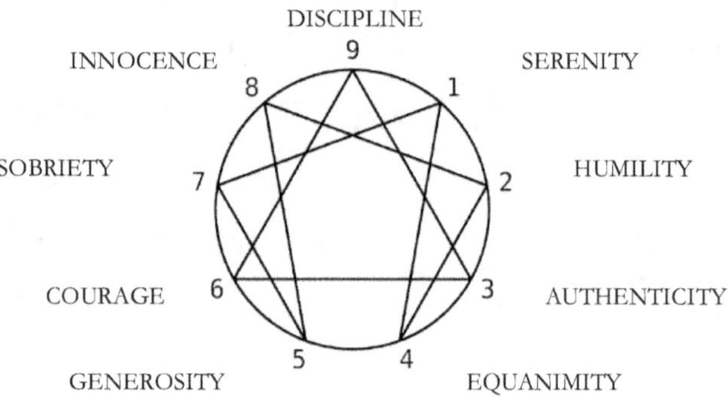

Steiner mentions a typical lamenting behavior labeled "Poor Me," which is characterized by playing the role of a victim who is searching for a savior: "She experiences some intimacy from putting herself in her 'Girl' state in relation to the 'Girl' state. 'Father' to others, but has rarely experienced intimacy on an equal level. By having permission to be childish, she can be spontaneous in a helpless, childish way and can invent many ways to act crazy.

She learns that she achieves things more easily by telling others about her problems, and thus she finds herself compelled not to abandon that image of herself. She spends a lot of time complaining about how horrible everything is, trying to get someone to do something about it. She continues to demonstrate that she is a victim, by creating situations in which she first manipulates others into doing something for her that

they really don't want to do, then feeling persecuted by them when they resent her." (Steiner: 1985).

The fourth type, like the second and third, is part of the so-called heart triad of the enneagram. Everyone struggles with the feeling that they can't be loved for who they are. The triad of feeling is "To feel or not to feel", acceptance is intrinsic in denial.

In the movie Mozart, Salieri is a Type 4 by being depressive, creative. He does not see his own gifts because of envy.

 **CHARACTERS FROM SERIES AND MOVIES**

In the "Grey's Anatomy" series, Meredith Grey is portrayed as a 4W5.

Meredith Gray is quite dramatic, intelligent, compassionate, hard-working, has good medical instincts and a natural gift for medicine. Meredith and Derek have been described as polar opposites. She described herself as "dark and twisted" due to her negativity, in contrast to Derek's charismatic optimism.

And unlike Derek, who saw the world in varying shades of black and white, Meredith tends to see things in shades of gray. She is unique, eccentric and different, always distinguished from others by her distinctive personality and aura.

In the movie "Gladiator", Commodus is a Type 4W3.

Photo taken from Netflix.

Commodus does not have any personal morals, principles or values. Although he is completely adaptable to the values of Roman society, his constant goal is to be admired, loved and accepted. Commodus is not mature enough.

He feels justified in his actions because he knows how to seduce others by knowing what they want in order to get their praise.

He is very insecure and questions his position among people. He has an appearance of intelligence; he is very good at scheming and plotting. Very conscious of his own image and enjoys the sensory world, although he has little understanding of his own emotions.

He is constantly speculating about things and objectively looking for possibilities that suit his desires. But also, he tends to be suspicious of situations that go against those speculations.

He has the great defects of Type 4, the great blind individuality

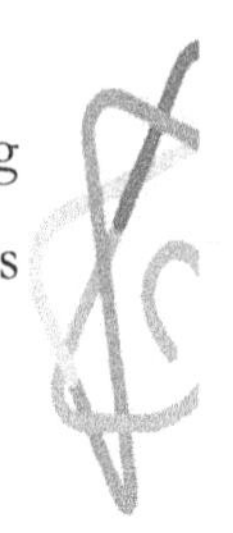

that makes him believe that he deserves everything, fantasizing in his actions, an intense emotionality and an envy of Maximus that in the end leads him to failure.

In the "Twilight" series, Edward Cullen is portrayed as a 4W5.

Edward has been waiting for something special for a hundred years. He is melancholic and very sensitive; he plays the piano during his long sleepless nights. He expresses his feelings easily, but with him everything is a drama.

ANALYSIS OF A BIBLICAL CHARACTER:

Examining Nicodemus, a biblical figure from the New Testament, we can identify elements suggesting that he could fit the Type 4 profile in the Enneagram.

Nicodemus Seeks Profound Understanding

In the Gospel of John, Nicodemus is introduced as a Pharisee and a member of the Sanhedrin, the Jewish ruling council. His first encounter with Jesus takes place at night, as recounted in John 3:1-2: "There was a man of the Pharisees named Nicodemus, a ruler of the Jews. This man came to Jesus by night and said to Him, 'Rabbi, we know that You are a teacher come from God; for no one can do these signs that You do unless God is with him.'"

Nicodemus's approach to Jesus in the darkness of night suggests a quest for meaning and a desire to deeply comprehend Jesus's teachings. Type 4 individuals are often introspective and long for a profound understanding of themselves and the world around them.

A Sense of Being Different and Special

Type 4 individuals frequently experience a sense of being unique and different from others. Nicodemus seems to share this feeling as he seeks out Jesus privately, avoiding public attention. His recognition of Jesus as someone "sent from God" might indicate a special connection that makes him feel different from others. Type 4 individuals seek authenticity and may feel they are unique and special in some way.

The Quest for Authenticity

The Type 4 struggle for authenticity and identity is a central feature. In John 3:3, Jesus responds to Nicodemus: "Jesus answered and said to him, 'Most assuredly, I say to you, unless one is born again, he cannot see the kingdom of God."

The concept of being "born again" is commonly interpreted as a spiritual rebirth, but it can also be understood as a process of self-discovery and personal transformation. Type 4 individuals often feel the need to reconnect with their true identity and find their place in the world, which aligns with Nicodemus's quest to understand the kingdom of God.

The Longing for Profound Experience

Type 4 individuals tend to seek deep experiences and emotions. In John 3:8, Jesus tells Nicodemus: "The wind blows where it wishes, and you hear the sound of it, but cannot tell where it comes from and where it goes. So is everyone who is born of the Spirit."

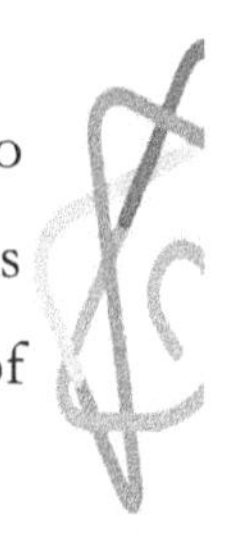

This metaphor of the wind can be interpreted as an invitation to experience the unknown and the profound. Type 4 individuals yearn for experiences and connections that provide a sense of meaning and authenticity.

The Struggle for Identity and Belonging

Nicodemus continues to appear in the Gospels, and his defense of Jesus before the Sanhedrin in John 7:50-51 is an example of his evolution: "Nicodemus, who came to Jesus by night, being one of them, said to them, 'Does our law judge a man before it hears him and knows what he is doing?'"

In this passage, Nicodemus defends Jesus and advocates for a fair trial. His willingness to take a stand and defend what he believes is right reflects a search for identity and belonging, characteristics of Type 4 in the Enneagram.

Nicodemus, through his actions and quests, can be seen as an exemplar of Type 4, "The Individualist" or "The Romantic," in the Enneagram. His pursuit of deep understanding, his sense of being unique, his yearning for authenticity, and his struggle for identity and belonging are elements that align with the characteristics of this personality type.

Try it for yourself

Maybe you belong to this Type 4, if you recognize the following:

☐ Do you have a tendency to long for what you feel is missing right now?

☐ Do you have great taste; do you like to be extraordinary and someone special?

☐ Do you often think about what others think of you and "read" their thoughts about you?

☐ Do you fight for what is missing through intense experience and creativity?

☐ Does ordinary life bore you?

☐ Do you usually try to diversify the routine and make it more exciting with the help of fantasies, creativity and dramatization of the imagination?

☐ Do you immerse yourself deeply in emotional experiences and have the ability to support others in times of crisis?

☐ Do you often have the desire to withdraw from social situations and feel like you don't fit in with the group?

Healthy Mode

Healthy Type 4s are idealists with a sense of taste and a great susceptibility to beauty. They filter external reality through their rich and sophisticated personal sense and have often developed metaphorical thinking, that is, the ability to connect separate facts and events. They know how to understand an event through the prism of another, see connection patterns in different situations.

This richness of perception is the raw material of creativity, and healthy Type 4s find their own way of expressing this intense inner life. When they write songs, compose poems and play roles; Somehow, they bring their feelings to a material support, and thus they can understand themselves better, "see" themselves from the outside. Not necessarily all Type Fours are creatives or actors, but in any job, they try to show their individuality.

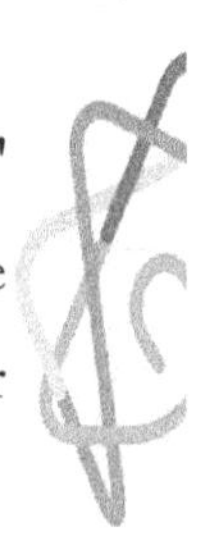

Healthy Type 4s are morally strong, idealistic, and work hard for what they believe in. They create more than they complain about and love to add a touch of originality to make the world a better place. Some 4s seek to realize their internal vision of the "ideal" world by creating innovative projects with humanistic or creative goals. They can be brave, determined and practical, and they don't want to waste their life on nonsense.

Passion Capital

The envy.

State of Stress, Unhealthy Mode or Disintegration from 4 to 2

If the Individualist is under pressure and feels insecure, then they begin to display Type 2 behavioral stereotypes. They lose touch with their emotions and become unsure of what they want. Unexpectedly for a Type 4, you find it easier to pay attention to other people's needs and begin to notice that you adapt to other people's desires. When their dreams and expectations are not fulfilled, they become angry with themselves out of shame, become depressed and emotionally paralyzed.

Security or Integration from 4 to 1

Being in a secure and resourceful state, Fours begin to display Type 1 behavior patterns. They are able to focus on the task and forget their concern for themselves. Thus, now Type 4 puts all its attention on the work. He pays more attention to details and likes to perfect everything. In an attempt to come into contact with more emotions, the sense of self becomes so strong that it withdraws from society and immerses itself in the self.

 ## Development and growth path for Type 4

You must rely on your special ability to perceive that everything around you is the same. To evaluate yourself and others without envy, you must pay attention to what is there now and realize that it is as valuable and attractive as what you currently lack. Paying more attention and appreciating the outside world more will help you achieve greater balance between that world and the inside. Learn to live more in the present and recognize the difference between real and idealized emotions.

Focus on what you already have (people around you, relationships) instead of looking at the flaws and lack of things and people. Because you tend to focus your attention on your own imaginary world, you can actively participate in society as a Healthy Type 1 by directing your attention to others and their interests.

When you focus on yourself, look at your strengths and the

positive aspects of what you've done. Doing so builds confidence. Keep in mind that the other person may not always understand you and may try to communicate with you frankly without getting emotional.

Vice

Envy is experienced as an inner emptiness, of loss.

 **How to communicate with a Type 4 person**

- Because Type 4s tend to enter the world of fantasy, the truly creative side of Fours can be revealed by supporting them to actively participate in the real world.

- By pointing out something, being too direct hurts Fours (due to their low self-esteem), so share your stance on deepening mutual understanding.

- Emotional expressions may be exaggerated at times, but accept them as they are. Show your willingness to support him at any time and show him that you want to understand him.

- Instead of looking at them with a relative feeling based on comparison with others, treat it with an absolute feeling that "because it's you" (special vision).

Fixation

Rich inner fantasies and a world of dreams, in comparison with which reality seems boring, something is missing in it. Type 4 flies towards idealized dreams or memories of the past.

Virtue

Equality is the desire for everyone to be equal in everything. Each person is equal and unique.

Creative Identity

Listening and Expression

Mood Intelligence

Those of Type 4 are related to Mental Intelligence, which is the ability to recognize what we want, and what excites us most. It is the power to guide our life in relation to our wants and desires. This intelligence allows us to "listen" to emotions that are loaded with information, to be able to live within them and come out when appropriate.

Keywords that symbolize Type 4

Unique, fantasies/delusions, sensitivity/aesthetics, shyness, melancholy, creativity, emotional richness, bad group behavior, intuition, tragic protagonist, self-expression, spirituality.

THE THINKER

Observer-Investigator
Enneatype 5

"I feel like I'm living an ordinary life, but both legs are off the ground."

Anonymous

 The observer has a great need for solitude. He protects himself from the intrusion of others. Type 5 is usually introverted, eccentric, perceptive, analytical, and busy thinking deeply about important issues or the state of the world.

Type 5 is a thinker, intelligent, logical, critical, original, patient, self-sufficient, independent and knowledgeable. He does not like working with others and has difficulty with authoritarian figures. The social role of a Type Five is "expert."

He is usually attentive, perceptive and curious. He wants to deeply understand what interests him, so he can focus and develop complex ideas and skills. Thus, he is concerned with the accumulation of knowledge because he loves to study, read, research and collect information.

"Don't ask me."

Carlos Naranjo comments: "The avoidance of commitment can also be considered as an expression of not giving, since it is due to the avoidance of having to give in the future. In this avoidance of commitment there is, however, another aspect: the need of Type 5 individuals to remain completely free, without limits, without impediments, in possession of the totality of themselves." (Naranjo: 1994).

Usually, observers are very sensitive people, but others often misinterpret their behavior as cold, because they do not show their emotions, but express themselves objectively and as if from the outside.

CAPITAL PASSIONS

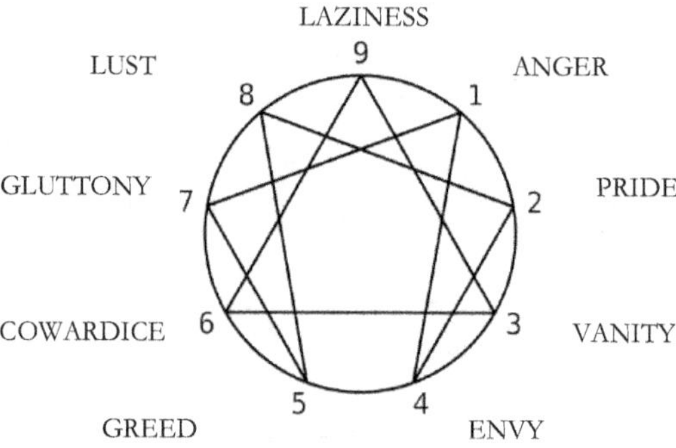

Type 5s are very rational and dispassionate. They have great interest in objectively understanding the reality of a society that surrounds them. They don't usually talk much about themselves or their emotions.

For example, on the streets of any of the major capitals, you can easily find yourself as a street artist making art with nature resources to sell to tourists. As a rule, he is silent, with a magnifying glass and completely immersed in his business. In this way, non-intellectual 5s develop rare and subtle abilities that help them stay apart from society and feel comfortable within their experience.

People of the fifth type can be called minimalists: they do not like clutter either in their work or in their personal life. Of the entire enneagram circle, this is the most introverted personality type.

It can be said that observers are stingy with their feelings. They experience emotions more easily when they are alone than with others.

Fives experience fear of confusion and emotions; the horror of being and the fear of being pressured. But even though Fives are afraid of emotions, one day they will trust you and allow you to come into their space and show strong emotions. Because they place too much importance on intelligence, they simulate situations in their heads and spend more time thinking before acting.

CHARACTERS FROM SERIES AND MOVIES

In the "Ertugrul" series, Emir Sadettin Köpek is portrayed as a 5W6.

Photo taken from Netflix.

The Emir represents excessive indulgence, hoarding, greed, the careful and secret accumulation of knowledge as power. The way he masters each specific thing, whether it be delicate wood carving or being a tasteful gourmet. He is rigid and completely self-controlled, unlike Type 3s, who tend to manipulate through charm and charisma. He has no charm or charisma, just a brilliant and intriguing detailed approach to chess-like power.

The Emir does not transform into an idealized version that others admire and does not seek to shine like the star in the eyes of the people. The Emir's motivation is to avoid the feeling of helplessness through the power of hoarding and knowledge, aided by mastery and self-control, which is the central motivation of a 5. Nothing escapes his sharp and laser-precise

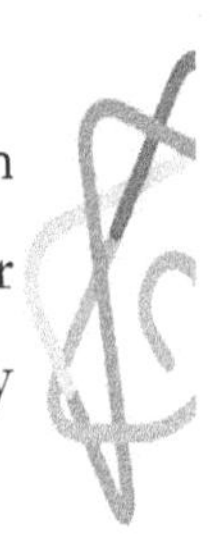

observation. Everything and everyone is a detailed mechanism to be controlled. He seeks to shore up and accumulate power through the precise gathering of knowledge that he carefully keeps to himself.

In the "Game of Thrones" series, Lord Varys is portrayed as a 5W6.

> "Power lies where you believe. It's a trick, a shadow on the wall."

Lord Varys is a eunuch who has served the kingdom since the Targaryen dynasty. Minister of Intelligence in King Robert's Small Council. Spies called "little birds" are deployed around the world to gather information not only about Westeros but also about Essos. A native of Essos, he was castrated as a child by a sorcerer. That's why he hates magic and witchcraft.

Always thinking of the people, he plots Daenerys' restoration of House Targaryen. He appreciates Tyrion's intelligence, and when he is found guilty of the murder of King Joffrey, he helps him and they head together to Essos. One of the main themes of Game of Thrones is power. Who has it, who wants it and who plays to hope for it.

In the "Twilight" series, Bella Swan is portrayed as a 5W4.
Bella is the type of person who goes unnoticed, she loves to

reflect and be alone. When her friends try on dresses, she prefers to go to a bookstore. She loves to investigate until she reaches total knowledge, which is how she discovers that Edward is a vampire. It is very difficult for her to express feelings; she does not get angry and avoids conflict. Bella has a large protective barrier against the outside, which means that not even Edward can read her thoughts.

ANALYSIS OF A BIBLICAL CHARACTER:

When we examine Lucas, one of the authors of the New Testament, we can identify traits that suggest he could align with the Type 5 profile in the Enneagram.

Lucas and his Pursuit of Knowledge

The Gospel according to Luke is renowned for its meticulous style and precise narration of events in Jesus's life. In his prologue (Luke 1:1-4, Reina Valera), Lucas states his intent to investigate and write accurately: "Since many have undertaken to set down an orderly account of the events that have been fulfilled among us, just as they were handed on to us by those who from the beginning were eyewitnesses and servants of the word, I too decided, after investigating everything carefully from the very first, to write an orderly account for you, most excellent Theophilus, so that you may know the truth concerning the things about which you have been instructed."

This prologue reveals Lucas's investigative nature. His desire to

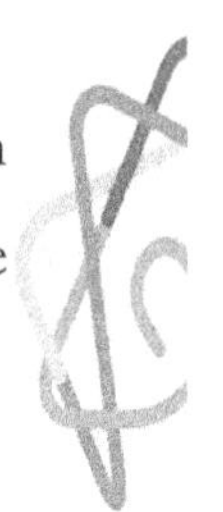

gather and present precise information suggests an affinity with the Type 5 of the Enneagram, which values in-depth knowledge and understanding.

Tendency Toward Observation and Reserve

Individuals of Type 5 are often meticulous observers and reserved. In Lucas's case, his detailed narration of events and his desire to present verified facts highlight his inclination toward meticulous observation. Furthermore, the fact that Lucas writes his Gospels objectively and without self-centeredness is characteristic of the Type 5's tendency to maintain personal reserve.

Energy Preservation

Type 5 seeks to preserve energy and limit draining social interactions. Lucas, in writing his Gospels, can be seen as exemplifying this characteristic of Type 5. Through his writing, he communicates his observations and knowledge without the need for extreme exposure or exhausting interpersonal interactions.

Deep Engagement with Religion and Spirituality

Type 5 often delves into profound and spiritual topics. In Lucas's case, his account of Jesus's birth, as well as his detailed descriptions of Jesus's teachings and miracles, indicate a deep interest in the spiritual and religious aspects of life. Lucas also stands out for including parables and narratives that reveal Jesus's understanding of human nature and spirituality.

Tendency to Store Knowledge

Type 5 tends to accumulate knowledge and be self-sufficient in their research. Lucas, as the author of the Gospel of Luke and the Acts of the Apostles, demonstrates his ability to gather information and present it coherently. His meticulous approach and his skill in narrating significant events in detail resonate with the nature of Type 5.

Lucas, through his work as the author of the Gospels and his focus on research and the objective presentation of events, can be identified as an example of Type 5 in the Enneagram, "The Investigator" or "The Observer." His quest for knowledge and precision, his penchant for meticulous observation, his personal reserve, his ability to conserve energy, and his interest in spiritual and religious subjects are elements that align with the characteristics of this personality type. Analyzing Lucas from the perspective of the Enneagram enriches our understanding of his contribution in the biblical context and his motivation as a writer.

Try it for yourself

Maybe you belong to this Type 5, if you recognize the following:

☐ Do you have a great need to be alone, even when you are in the company of other people?

☐ Are you busy collecting information and want to have the key to understanding the world?

☐ Do you like to plan everything and prepare yourself mentally to avoid surprises?

☐ Can you get by on little because your requests for basic needs are small?

☐ You can go to a party, but you will only truly experience it when you remember it, having already returned home?

☐ Is it like you're not here if there are a lot of people around you?

☐ Do you have the ability to be objective and do not allow other people's opinions or needs to influence you?

☐ Do you value the right to privacy and never reveal someone else's secret?

Healthy Mode

Healthy Type 5s typically have a well-developed ability to gather and synthesize knowledge. These are "forever" learners who remain mentally alive and interested well into their later years. Type 5s can be receptive, wise, and objective, and can remain calm in situations where everyone else is confused and panicked. At their best, Type 5s maintain a balance between engaging with the world and withdrawing from it. This type is associated with competent knowledge and sometimes intellectual genius.

For many, the life motto of Type Fives is "knowledge is power." And at healthy levels, Type 5s actively offer the fruits of their interest and research to the world. It's as if they believe they should dedicate their teaching talents to the greater good for many people. There are notes of idealism and desire to contribute to the common cause in this.

They can also be trusted and humble behind-the-scenes partners who don't step into the spotlight but can support and revitalize the efforts of the entire group. While Type Fives are generally mind controlled, not all are scientific intellectuals.

Healthy Type 5s can play the games of life without being attached to their results. They involve themselves fully and with dignity in events, but they do not take them personally and without bad intentions.

Healthy Type Fives sympathize with the suffering of others and are often kind. As friends, they can be incredibly tolerant, able to accept oddities and moral errors without judgment. Type 5s can also consider a wide variety of points of view and understand them all.

Daniel L. Everett comments: "I became convinced that I was in the happiest town on Earth and also one where the people were more supportive and benevolent than in any known Christian town. [...] They are also the most benevolent and most willing to forgive offenses or attacks. " (Everett: 2014).

Passion Capital
Greed.

State of Stress, Unhealthy Mode or Disintegration from 5 to 7

When Type Fives are under pressure and feel their boundaries are being violated, they gain access to stereotypes of Type 7 behavior. They lose their inner balance and become overwhelmed by unrealistic ideas, leading Observers into a state of uncertainty.

They begin to deal with problems superficially and become extroverted. This gives them the feeling that they do not respect themselves or those around them. They isolate themselves from the real world when they become hermits, nihilists and refuse to belong to society.

Security or Integration from 5 to 8

When observers feel confident and secure, they gain access to Type 8 behavior patterns. They begin to command more, easily taking control into their own hands. It's now easy for them to make sure your needs are met, and they can be very charming.

The Five's usual strategy is just thinking about something is replaced by action. They observe all phenomena with heightened insight, see through the essence of things and leave behind innovative and outstanding achievements as an expert in their field.

Development and growth path for Type 5

By generously sharing resources, you open up an inexhaustible source of knowledge and energy. Then it makes it possible for you to establish a connection with a special manifestation of the true essence.

You must understand that there is more value in learning through practical experience and real feelings than learning through the collection and analysis of mental knowledge. Regular physical activity can help you feel connected to your body, leading to the confidence and deep strength of a healthy Type Eight.

Asking for help and expressing your feelings openly helps you connect with others. You tend to give up quickly, but by facing your emotions, you develop the ability to take on difficult challenges.

Vice

Greed feels like a lack or limitation of available resources of energy, knowledge, space and love.

 ## How to communicate with a Type 5 person

If Type 5s have an advisory role at work it highlights their strengths in information gathering and objectivity. They tend to hoard information, so ask and trust Type 5s. That way you can gain valuable knowledge.

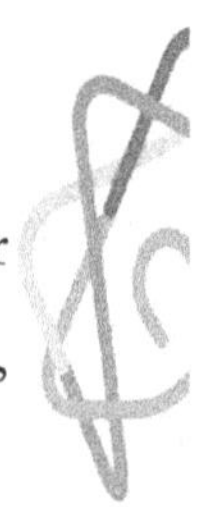

They need time to think, so you should wait without asking for a quick response. When you have a disagreement with a Type 5, try to speak logically, without getting emotional.

Fixation

Stealth/Seclusion: It is a reaction to limited resources that causes Type 5 to appreciate what they have and thus avoid situations where others around them are waiting for something, because this means they will have to lose some of their accumulated resources.

Virtue

Generosity is experienced as a strong emotional love towards people and the world, through which Type Five sacrifices time and resources to create something good in the world.

Competition and Wisdom

Live good.

Rational Intelligence

Those of Type 5 are related to Rational Intelligence, which is based on reason and leads to understandings that go beyond experience; Therefore, analogy and deduction become fundamental tools that promote learning. It is correlated with the joy of knowledge and all truly valid knowledge that produces inner exaltation. Rational Intelligence is not based on the art of finding answers but on the art of asking the right questions. Rational Intelligence leads to understanding the why of things, which is why it grants respect to those who truly know.

Keywords that symbolize Type 5

Objective (observant), Calm and Serene, Professionalism, Indifference to emotions, Indifference, Difficulty socializing, Give up quickly, Reflective, Logical, Knowledgeable, not good at the unexpected, Loneliness.

THE LOYALIST

Loyal-Skeptic
Enneatype 6

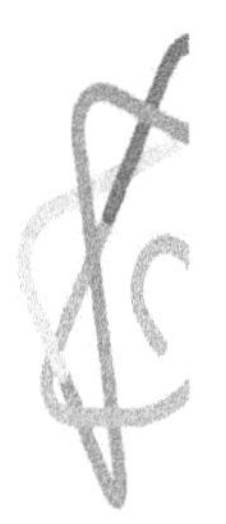

"Three experienced pilots watch as the plane takes off directly into the storm. One says: "There goes a daredevil." Second: "Here's an idiot taking off." And the third: "I don't see any difference between them."

Anonymous

 The Loyal is dutiful, dependent, kind and masochistic. He is guided by the principle of "you never know when anything can go wrong" and often represents the worst-case scenario. The fundamental issue for him is communication with fear.

Type 6 fights fear by succumbing to it or acting against it. It can be said that there are Type Six phobics who avoid people and anything that scares them; and there are Type Sixes against phobics who specifically choose what they fear (risking).

The phobic Type 6, in a dangerous situation, behaves cautiously, silently and accommodating to avoid a possible attack. The counterphobic, on the other hand, provokes and shows aggression even more, to confront the problem before the problem "confronts" him.

The phobic Type 6 is charming, humble, gentle and his motto is "Fear, go away." And the counterphobic, on the contrary, looks cold, defiant and caustic with a motto: "Fear is never boring!" There are people with a pronounced polarity, but most Type 6s fall somewhere between these two extremes, and in different situations they display phobic or counterphobic traits.

Type 6 has a tendency to abide by the rules and question all the logic of action that derives from them. If he is freed from these rules, he becomes very insecure and falls into constant doubt.

Type 6 people are concerned with security and authority. They avoid boasting about themselves because it is more convenient for them when they are barely noticeable. Loyalists have a hard time believing in others and have developed a special ability to "see through" what moves "within an individual."

They analyze the situation well in search of possible risks. They are good at seeing any scenario from a different perspective. They are very devoted to people who have earned their trust.

"Don't let them fool me."

Type Sixes are intuitive, serious, self-sacrificing and imaginative.

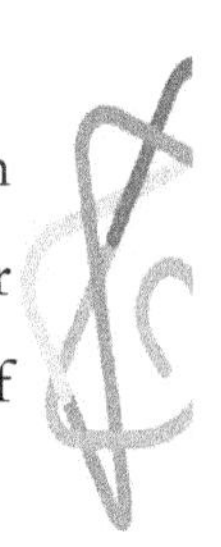

However, they have few friends and are very loyal to those with whom they seek to have a long relationship. They work better under pressure, fear direct anger, and distrust the motives of others, so they seek protection in the social structure.

The sixth type enters into alliances with authoritarian people and always calculates actions a few steps ahead. The deepest fear is being unprepared and unable to defend oneself from danger. Skeptics are constantly strategizing and planning for the future to protect themselves and their loved ones from harm.

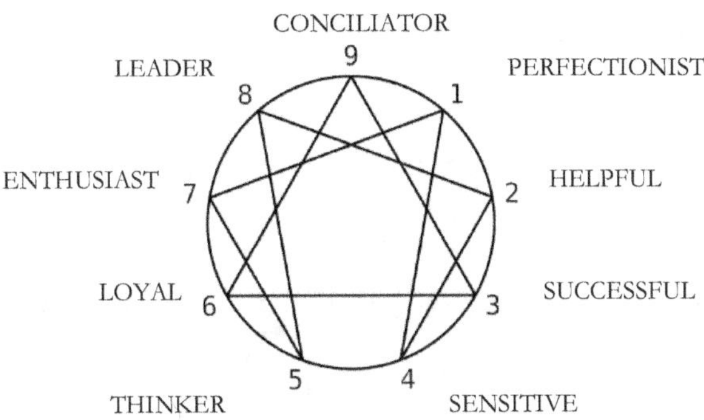

Type 6s have great difficulty in business and setting goals, due to strong self-doubt. They constantly ask themselves questions and thinking slows them down. Consequently, ambivalence and procrastination arise day by day. They long to talk non-stop and point out what is false.

Negative memories are more accessible than positive ones. They like to follow rules to feel safe. They become indecisive, afraid to make decisions because of their underlying insecurities.

They are masochists because they test you to see how much you love them and to what extent you put a stop to it. Then Type 6s feel guilty about what they do and think that they must be punished to atone for their sins and thus test you again if you are going to abandon them.

Horney called a masochistic character, in which there is a poor self-image, a predisposition to suffer more than necessary, a great dependence on the love of others, a feeling of chronic rejection and a tendency to dissatisfaction. (Horney:1990).

 ## CHARACTERS FROM SERIES AND MOVIES

In the "Yo soy, Betty la Fea" series, Betty is portrayed as a 6W5.

Betty uses her past experiences to focus her future and is distrustful of those who hurt her in the past. When Daniel asks her out, she is hostile because of all the bad things he said to her previously. She gains self-confidence through alliances with her friends while carrying out her work with professionalism and loyalty, saving the company from various problems and swallowing her pride. Betty is afraid of change.

"So divine"

This phrase was used by the women of Ecomoda to refer to a handsome man. Betty used to use it when Don Armando had a detail with her.

"My beauty is natural."

It was the expression used by Betty when they made fun of her physical beauty.

In the "Friends" series, Chandler Bing is portrayed as a 6W7.

Photo taken from NBC.

Chandler is observant, non-judgmental and naturally considers the variables around him. He is skeptical and focused on routine. It is not a question of insecurity; it is a natural closure to the environment. He is a social introvert, appearing open and curious, desiring social interaction but unwilling to actively light up the social atmosphere. He often likes to have someone more outgoing to break the ice and make comments.

"Hi, I'm Chandler and I make jokes when I'm uncomfortable."

Chandler becomes anxious and compensates with excess humor. An example is when he starts smoking again and uses the group's flaws to do some manipulation and distract them from themselves. Another example is when he avoids exercising with Monica, showing her how he compensates for his loneliness with training and convinces her to go to bed and rest. Chandler is also quite desperate to maintain harmony in the group and his jokes serve as a way to achieve this. Chandler is sometimes willing to do acts that embarrass him to make people laugh. His career in advertising also reflects his ability and willingness to engage people and work for a group.

"I'm not good at advising... Can I interest you in a sarcastic comment?"

He makes friends easily, behaving warmly with others and thus lifts their spirits. It is difficult to get to know him because when he feels uncomfortable around him, he appears disinterested with others. Avoidant and distant. One of his main problems, as a person, is his inability to stop feeling uncomfortable and distant with others. The way he jokes, he gets tense at the worst possible

times.

He loves parties and group activities and likes to involve others, although he avoids crowds. Prefers tranquility and solitude. He likes being in his small circle and feels moderately comfortable, especially with Joey, with whom he feels the need to constantly work on their friendship.

He lets a coworker mistakenly refer to him for years and is afraid to take the initiative in his own relationships. He also doesn't want to confront his own parents about his misdeeds. Chandler only cares about his job and relationships, and often even feels constantly lost and bored when he is not employed. He tends to prefer slower-moving environments and people, and may become overwhelmed when he feels that his surroundings or friends are moving too quickly. Chandler is a Type 6 who prefers to stick to what he knows, again, hence his commitment issues and general fear of making consequential mistakes, or fear of things just "going wrong." Chandler tries to compensate for his feelings of inferiority or discomfort by trying to entertain and uplift the people around him with positivity and humor.

In the "Harry Potter" series, Severus Snape is portrayed as a 6W5.

Severus adopts a dominant stance, attacking before he can be attacked, using intimidation as a defense mechanism, and projecting this lack of trust onto others. From his approach to things, intellectually and verbally, to his wardrobe choices, Snape seeks to command respect, be feared, and directly initiate conflict at all times.

Severus was severely bullied growing up and never knew kindness or calm at home. You can clearly see how it has affected him, because of the way he takes on challenges immediately if you call him a "coward" or the way he suddenly bullies and humiliates Harry Potter. Harry's appearance alone reminds him of his childhood bully, James Potter. Harry is not only the lookalike, but also the infinite reminder that "the love of his life" chose James, his bully, over him, therefore, Snape projects this mentality of not being good enough on those around him, especially his enemies, always taking a direct and confrontational approach and never allowing anyone to underestimate him again.

Another example is his desperation to expose Remus Lupine and get him fired, or catch Sirius Black, as revenge for their childhood fights. Snape's behavior is a result of the past making him always on guard. His loyalty lies where his sexuality and affection lie, with the memory of Lily, who had all his loyalty for the simple fact that she was the only one who showed him kindness and acceptance.

Snape has a natural ability to see patterns, make connections, and predict the future. This cognitive function is evident throughout the Harry Potter series, giving Snape an advantage in many situations. For example, in the first film, "Harry Potter and the Philosopher's Stone," Snape was able to deduce that someone was trying to steal the Philosopher's Stone and set in motion a series of events that ultimately saved the wizarding world. Throughout the series, Snape's ability to predict the future and anticipate the actions of others is also evident in his role as a spy. As a member of both the Order of the Phoenix and the Death Eaters, he walks a fine line between loyalties, always seeming to be one step ahead of everyone else.

Another example of Snape is his ability to plan and strategize. As a brew master at Hogwarts, Snape is known for his ability to carefully evaluate and plan his moves. This cognitive function allows him to create complex potions, such as the Draft of Living Death, a concoction that puts the drinker into a deep, death-like sleep, and develops the antidote to cure all poisons, an option that can counter, even, the most devastating effects.

Snape values the feelings of others and is able to empathize with those around him. This is evident in his interactions with other characters in the Harry Potter series, where he often shows concern and compassion for his loved ones.

Throughout the films, Snape's ability to empathize with others is evident in his love for Lily Evans, deep guilt over her death, and continued protection of his son, Harry Potter. Despite his cold and distant exterior, Snape maintains his loyalty to Albus

Dumbledore and the Order of the Phoenix. He is willing to do anything to protect the magical world and the people in it, even if it means sacrificing his own life. This is evident in his role as a spy, where he is willing to play the role of a Death Eater to protect Dumbledore. Despite his difficult past and cold demeanor, Snape is able to form close relationships with others, such as with Harry Potter, whom he ultimately sacrifices everything to protect.

In the "The Walking Dead" series, Eugene Porter is portrayed as a 6W5.

Photo taken from Netflix.

Eugene is an extremely mentally weak person who bonds with specific individuals who are strong, for example. Abraham, Rosita and then Negan. He provides useful services to others through his intelligence due to his ability to plan ahead, learn and gather information and then apply that research to make things more effective.

He is a man embodied in his careful nature, logical perspective, and vast amounts of incredibly detailed frameworks and knowledge. Eugene has a lot of trouble adapting and solving problems because of how specific his knowledge and logic is.

Eugene faces fear and defends himself with barricades. He literally refused to stab the walkers, leaving it to the others. It's the way he entrenched himself from the apocalypse. The "You're screwed either way. " Tara was the one who brought him out of that shell. Being competent is what it is based on. Intellectualism, intellectual snobbery, and zero self-awareness work much better with him.

ANALYSIS OF A BIBLICAL CHARACTER:

When scrutinizing Joseph, as per the biblical account, Mary's husband, we can identify traits hinting at his alignment with the Type 6 profile in the Enneagram.

Joseph and his Pursuit of Security

In the narrative of Jesus's birth in the Gospel of Matthew, Joseph grapples with the news that Mary, his betrothed, is pregnant before they live together as husband and wife. In Matthew 1:20-21 (Reina Valera), an angel of the Lord appears to him in a dream to allay his fears:

"But while he thought on these things, behold, the angel of the

Lord appeared unto him in a dream, saying, 'Joseph, thou son of David, fear not to take unto thee Mary thy wife: for that which is conceived in her is of the Holy Ghost. And she shall bring forth a son, and thou shalt call his name Jesus: for he shall save his people from their sins.'"

Joseph's initial concern and need for security are reflected in his reaction to the angel's message. This episode suggests that Joseph could possess traits of the Type 6 in the Enneagram, which often seeks security and protection.

The Propensity for Scrutiny and Preparedness

Individuals of Type 6 tend to be cautious and anticipate potential dangers. Joseph, faced with the unusual situation of Mary's pregnancy, can be viewed as an example of this Type 6 tendency. Although initially concerned, his willingness to heed the angel's counsel and marry her signifies an attitude of scrutiny and preparedness to confront the unknown.

The Need for Guidance and Support

Type 6 individuals often seek guidance and support from authority figures or sources of security. In Joseph's case, his readiness to embrace the angel's guidance reflects this need for divine support and direction in a time of uncertainty. Type 6 individuals tend to turn to authority figures to feel secure and protected.

Loyalty and Commitment

Type 6 values loyalty and commitment in relationships. Despite his initial doubts, Joseph displays ongoing commitment to Mary and baby Jesus. In Matthew 1:24-25 (Reina Valera), we read:

"Then Joseph being raised from sleep did as the angel of the Lord had bidden him, and took unto him his wife: And knew her not till she had brought forth her firstborn son: and he called his name Jesus."

Joseph's decision to accept Mary as his wife and raise baby Jesus as his own son showcases his loyalty and commitment, characteristic of Type 6.

Joseph, through his initial concerns and his quest for security through the angel's message, can be identified as an example of Type 6 in the Enneagram, "The Loyal" or "The Skeptic." His need for security, his willingness to scrutinize and prepare for challenges, his quest for guidance and support, and his loyalty and commitment to Mary and Jesus are elements that align with the characteristics of this personality type.

Try it for yourself

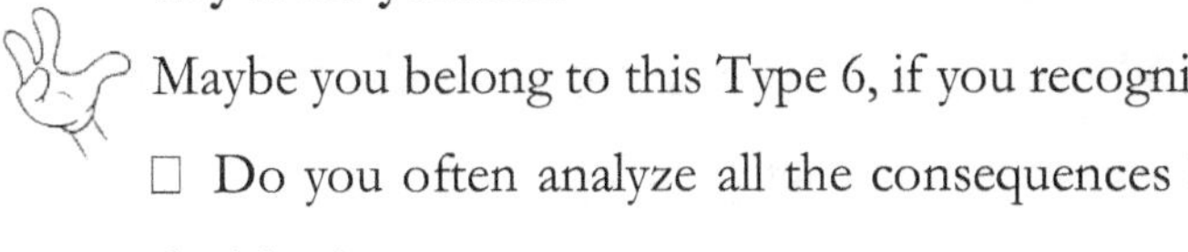

Maybe you belong to this Type 6, if you recognize the following:

☐ Do you often analyze all the consequences before making a decision?

☐ Authority figures are important in your life, or are you with them or against them?

☐ Do you identify with the "just cause" and protect the unfortunate and weak?

☐ Are you often skeptical and think "yes, but..." or "if it's the other way around..."?

☐ Do you have the habit of wondering if your decision was the right one?

☐ Are you looking for hidden intentions that could affect cooperation?

☐ Are you very devoted to your friends and do you firmly support them?

☐ Are you trying to balance opinions by expressing the opposite point of view?

Healthy Mode

Healthy phobic 6s are stable, loyal and idealistic. They embody the "truth of commitment," but they do so by choice and with total dedication. They are often loyal to a group, tradition, or idea, keep their promises, work hard, and are respectful and protective friends. A perfect example of this type is Robert De Niro's character in The Intern (2015).

Healthy phobic Type 6s are also diplomatic and courteous. They communicate with people with ease, prudence and pleasant manners, being very fun and imaginative.

They can be very fair leaders who sympathize with weak team

members and help all people show their strengths. But at the same time, they do not forget about their personal value to the team and can make unpopular decisions. In general, they work toward the goals of the entire group, allowing everyone to feel victory.

Healthy Type 6 anti-phobics are very brave and can even grab a tiger by the tail, being adventurous, very capable and truly enjoying life. They treat traditions from the position of constructive criticism, creating something new on the basis of the old and offering new alternatives to the team. They are energetic, honest, assertive people, with good ideas, who work as a team.

At their best, antiphobic Type 6s are creative and original. They know how to see beyond the surface and not believe in hasty conclusions, so their opinions are usually deep and insightful. They often engage in creativity and find their strength in it. In general, these people are hardworking, loyal, and highly idealistic.

Passion Capital

The fear.

 **State of Stress, Unhealthy Mode or Disintegration from 6 to 3**

When Type 6 is under pressure or something threatens them, they begin to use behavioral stereotypes of Type 3. They become more active, but at the same time they feel frustrated because they are not able to think deeply about what is happening before taking action. a decision. Driven by anxiety, they underestimate themselves and become extremely dependent on others.

Security or Integration from 6 to 9

When the Loyal feels safe and trustworthy, he uses Type 9 behaviors, slows down and begins to accept what is and see people as mostly good. Skepticism recedes, in its place comes the feeling: "it is better to just enjoy each other's company."
He becomes a sincere person, who trusts in himself and others, has a sense of responsibility, values his family, friends and the organization to which he belongs.

Development and growth path for Type 6

It consists of getting rid of doubts and developing confidence, this will allow you to access such a manifestation of the essence, in which the belief that "everything is fine" is strong.

If you have a concern, don't overthink it, talk frankly to someone you trust and get advice. When you have a vague problem, separate the facts from the interpretation (imagination). You often worry about things that are not true.

Actively increase positive time, such as playing and having fun from the bottom of your heart. This will develop a great ability to support others.

Vice

Fear: not felt directly, but manifests as a state of constant anxiety and apprehension. Subconscious motivation: feeling of danger.

How to communicate with a Type 6 person

Type 6s are always observant and have a good eye for what others really think, so ask them. Unexpected compliments, on the other hand, make the other person skeptical.

Type 6s respect superiors and people in leadership positions, but at the same time they see them as too big, so you should be careful when calling them out.

Fixation

Doubt controls the mind. Type 6 constantly analyzes and finds contradictions in their own and other people's opinions, intentions, and incompetence.

Virtue

Courage is a great inner strength to act despite all the internal uncertainty: courage must make you believe that everything is fine.

Associative Intelligence

Those of Type 6 are related to Associative Intelligence whose ability is to link or relate to that which wants to be associated. They have the ability to combine, associate information or interact through random thought connections. The difficulty is not being able to reach a decision or conclusion. In personal life we apply it respecting the thoughts expressed by other people and in the workplace, we use it in innovation and synergy between co-workers. Associative Intelligence promotes understanding and good interpersonal relationships at work; Additionally, execute tasks and activities as a team to obtain goals and better results.

Keywords that symbolize Type 6

Anxious, Suspicious, Security Seeker, Kindness, Friendship, Compliance with rules, Loyalty to the group, Dependent, Contradictory with oneself, Sarcastic humor, Sensitive to the intentions of others, Responsibility.

THE GENERALIST

Enthusiast-Outburst
Enneatype 7

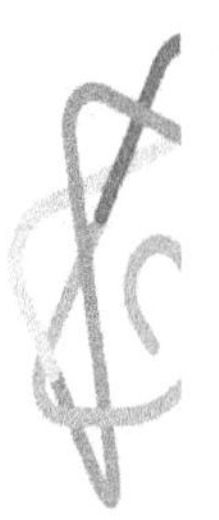

"I want to be an example for my children. And when I die, they won't know about me that I would like to live my life differently. I'm a big Yes."

Anonymous

 Enthusiasts are driven by everything new and inspiring. Type 7 personalities see the glass "half full" and perceive the world as an unlimited field of possibilities. They are impulsive, excessive, accomplished and manic people. They love to create fantastic plans, and not necessarily implement them at all. They actively display enthusiasm, which others may perceive as superficial. They plan well, moving toward future opportunities and pleasures; most of their enthusiasm is related to the beginning of the projects and less to the continuation.

"Don't leave me alone."

They are concerned with joy, pleasure, and having more options; which causes them to frequently abandon their long-term goals. They tend to display good humor and reject the possibility of making a commitment so as not to have to mourn losses.

They avoid hurting each other with memories or emotions and any type of commitment that remotely feels like a trap. Their main defense is overindulgence and rationalization. Their main problem is the fear of deprivation, which they evade with the help of excessive indulgence and activities that bring pleasure. Sevens are adventurous and versatile, creative thinkers, extroverted, popular and self-sufficient. They love parties and tend to be the center of attention at them. They have little or no self-discipline. Dreams and fantasies are much more attractive than reality.

DIFFERENT TYPES OF INTELLIGENCES

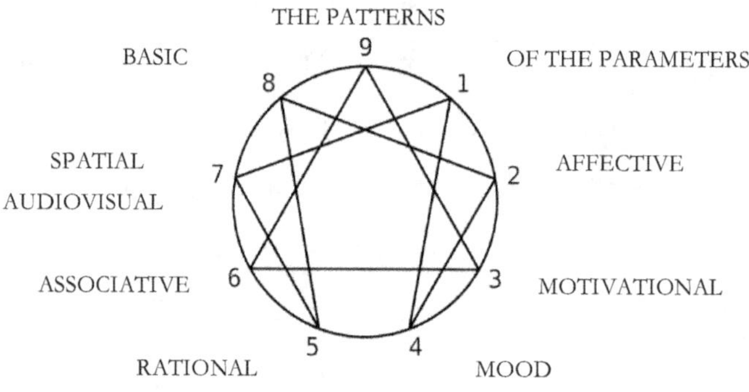

Type Sevens tend to exist on the run, at a fast pace and escaping boredom in all directions. They are selfish, rebellious, dreamers and deny that they have any problems, especially emotional ones. Type 7s have a tendency to perceive life as a pleasure, which masks their deep emotions. They have many relationships and

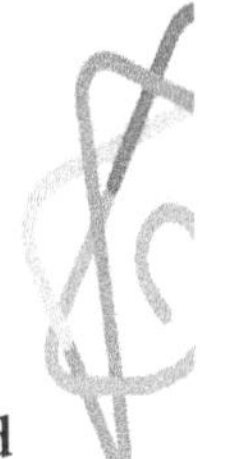

careers.

CHARACTERS FROM SERIES AND MOVIES

In the "Billions" series, Mike "Wags" Wagner is portrayed as a 7W8.

Photo taken from Netflix.

Wags is perhaps Bobby's most trusted partner and confidant. He is deeply loyal to his boss and says several times that he owes him his life. At the office, he often acts as Ax Capital's leader in Bobby's absence.

Wags is a ruthless trader and verbally abuses many Ax Capital employees, saying that it motivates them, although he admits that he also enjoys it. This goes along with his tendency to overreact and his taste for theatrics. He frequently employs large images in his rants and quotes books, movies, and famous historical figures for dramatic effect.

Although Wags is loyal to Bobby and his friends, he is often incredibly mean and disrespectful to everyone else he encounters. In one case, he hatches a plan against an employee who had asked for a raise or threatened to leave. Wags admits to Wendy, the HR manager, that while he believes she deserved the raise and is a good employee, he was offended by her threat to leave unless Wags gave him the raise.

He details to Wendy his plan to give her the raise and slowly reduce the capital she can invest, eventually reducing her salary to nothing. In another case, he employs Hall's spies to publicly reveal a lawyer's crumbling marriage because he purchased a burial plot that Wags had planned to acquire.

Witty and foul-mouthed, Wags has an abiding, occasionally out-of-control enthusiasm for the finer things in life, legal and otherwise. His joy at living alone is matched by his fierce attack-dog devotion to his friend and boss, Bobby Axelrod, and the jaunty curl of his devilish mustache.

Wags is a dandy from the Wall Street underworld. Aside from all that debauchery, he's a guy who's vital for inviting big clients or investors to expense account dinners, or Las Vegas meetings, or inappropriate gentlemen's clubs. When it comes down to it, he has to know what he is doing at the negotiating table or else it would all be in vain. He is a smart and experienced guy who has survived everything, knows how to bond with a great trader as his leader and support him as the best number two on Wall

Street.

Recognizes and respects passion, art and beauty. Money is really in the service of something much bigger. For example, there is beauty in the world and there are many forms of love. Certainly, Eros is preferred, but erotic love, not only of another person, but of the world, of food, of eroticism itself. You see it in everything he is: the way he moves, the clothes he wears. He loves excess.

The scene in the cemetery is a real and direct path to what we are talking about here. "The idea that in Wags' mind, if you're alive, you might as well live."
Wags is someone very aware of his mortality. It lives for those extreme moments and its dimmers are only fully on during the most intense moments.

Wags attempts to mend his estranged relationships with his adult children by trying to make a new baby and do everything right from the beginning. However, this being Wags, there's more to this scheme than simply getting back into the parenting game: Chelsea, the woman he chooses as his future mother, is also the daughter of an old enemy.

Wags decides that his parenting has not been a great success due to his past of partying and drinking too much. He maintains a faith that as long as he is there, he can do well and can continue to commit with his entire being.

In the movie "Scarface", Manny Rivera is a Type 7W6.

Foto tomada de Netflix

Although Manny is a Type 7, he tries to avoid conflict and establish peace between people by making deals whenever possible. You can see this when Omar offered him the first deal and they were working at the restaurant. Aside from the fact that his morality does not seem to be purely individual, he sees laws as universals that apply to everyone. Examples of this are him showing Tony what "the perfect way" to pick up girls in the United States is. Manny can look a little wary when Gina, Tony's sister, asks him why he doesn't ask her out on a date. In the bathtub scene, he shows us how his motivation, sentimentality and optimism work. Comparing him to Tony, Manny sounds a bit witty and dumb. He's a character who looks chaotic most of the time and then shoots someone randomly and smiles.

In the "Star Wars" series, Han Solo is portrayed as a 7W8.

> "The outside looks like a mess, but it's the inside that counts."

It is a wild date in the style of Han Solo, who is opportunistic and has to find advantages, to profit. It is as if a threat to conservation hangs over it that must be compensated. He does business instantly because his mind is so alert to opportunities that he never misses them. His position is that of someone who thinks that if you are not alert, if you do not keep your nose in touch with the wind to take advantage of opportunities, you will be a loser.

Han Solo is charming, bold and energetic. He's not one to sit around debating the meaning of life, he prefers to be out there taking action and having adventures. Han Solo is certainly ambitious, loves challenges and values his freedom, avoiding situations in which he feels tied down. Han Solo lives in the moment and is very observant of his surroundings, noticing details that very few capture. As a result, Han Solo is keen to detect changes in body language and tone of voice. He has a unique ability to remain calm in stressful situations.

No one commands him, nor is he a self-initiated leader, he simply mobilizes people to take practical action when they need it. Han Solo is very grounded in reality and only takes those actions that have great returns. He's the guy who likes to play it safe, rarely taking risks unless they guarantee him an outcome:

money. He acts as the leader of the ship many times because it is his job to do so. He also doesn't try too hard for a specific goal or vision; he just takes life for what it is and lives it.

"What is for me?".

Han Solo tries to maximize practical results with little to no focus on power dynamics, only using force because he has to and because it comes naturally to him to do so. Han Solo's biggest struggle is expressing his emotions and acting on the feelings of others. Han is rough, unfiltered and blunt to a fault.

In the "Money Heist" series, Denver is portrayed as a 7W6. Denver is enthusiastic, optimistic, spontaneous, playful and often seeks out new and stimulating experiences. He tends to be impulsive, but he is also happy and very grateful.

"Sooner or later... everything ends."

In the "Fast & Furious" series, Brian O'Conner is portrayed as a 7W8.

Photo taken from Universal Studios.

Brian fits into this Type 7 because they are the ones who love adrenaline. He is introverted, brave and tough. Brian is not your average cop; He's been on the other side of the law long enough to understand what drives people to become criminals. His tough personality is what earns him Toretto's respect. As he announced in his first street race:

"If I lose, the winner gets my clean car. But if I win, I take the money and I take the respect."

In the "Game of Thrones" series, Tyrion Lannister is portrayed as a 7W6.

Photo taken from HBO.

"Your joy will turn to ashes in your mouth."

It's what Tyrion Lannister said when he took revenge on Cersei and you could feel the energetic, stimulating desire for revenge.

Tyrion is an intelligent and talkative dwarf. During his trial, which he did not win, he said: "I wish I were the monster you think I am" and goes on to say: "I am innocent, but I have been found guilty because of the body I possess." With this last sentence, you can feel Tyrion's dissatisfaction and hatred towards the court's verdict. It is a quote that only he, who has been discriminated against for being a dwarf, can say.

"I have a tenderness in my heart for cripples, bastards and broken things."

The previous expression was said by Tyrion to Brandon Stark at the beginning of the series.

"Never forget who you are. The rest of the world won't. Wear it like armor and never use it to hurt yourself."
Tyrion is here to give Jon Snow some sage advice, demonstrating his great capacity for wisdom and psychological insight.

"That's my job: drink and find out."
Tyrion is intelligent, ruthless, but above all witty and self-critical.

ANALYSIS OF A BIBLICAL CHARACTER:

When analyzing Peter, one of Jesus's most prominent apostles, we can identify traits suggesting that he could align with the Type 7 profile in the Enneagram.

Peter and His Optimistic Nature

Peter, in his numerous encounters and discussions with Jesus, often displays an optimistic and enthusiastic attitude. In the Gospel of Matthew 16:16, when Jesus asks his disciples who they say He is, Peter responds enthusiastically:

> "And Simon Peter answered and said, 'Thou art the Christ, the Son of the living God.'"

This response showcases Peter's willingness to embrace belief in something grand and transcendent, characteristic of Type 7 in the Enneagram, which tends to focus on the positive and exciting.

Aversion to Limitations and Varied Experiences

Type 7 individuals often avoid limitations and seek varied and exciting experiences. Throughout his association with Jesus, Peter seeks to live diverse and exciting experiences. An example of this is when he walks on water in Matthew 14:28-29, at the invitation of Jesus:

> "And Peter answered him and said, 'Lord, if it be thou, bid me come unto thee on the water.' And he said, 'Come.' And when Peter was come down out of the ship, he walked on the water, to go to Jesus."

Peter's willingness to venture out of his comfort zone and walk on water reflects his readiness to embrace exciting and challenging experiences, consistent with Type 7's nature.

Tendency to Avoidance and Positivity

Type 7 often tends to avoid pain and negativity, striving to maintain a positive focus. In the moment of Jesus's betrayal and arrest, Peter attempts to avoid facing the negative situation. In Matthew 26:51-54, we read about his reaction to Jesus's arrest:

"And, behold, one of them which were with Jesus stretched out his hand, and drew his sword, and struck a servant of the high priest's, and smote off his ear. Then said Jesus unto him, 'Put up again thy sword into his place: for all they that take the sword shall perish with the sword. Thinkest thou that I cannot now pray to my Father, and he shall presently give me more than twelve legions of angels?'"

Peter tries to avoid negative confrontation and reacts impulsively, suggesting his tendency to maintain a positive focus and avoid emotional pain.

Pursuit of Freedom and Difficulty with Commitments

Type 7 often seeks freedom and struggles with long-term commitments. Peter, in various biblical passages, demonstrates his inclination to pursue freedom and grapple with commitments. For example, when he denies Jesus three times before the rooster crows, he reflects his difficulty in maintaining

a commitment in a moment of crisis.

Peter, through his optimistic attitude, pursuit of exciting experiences, aversion to negativity, and difficulty with commitments, can be identified as an example of Type 7 in the Enneagram, "The Enthusiast" or "The Epicure." His willingness to embrace the exciting and the positive, his quest for variety, and his struggle to face negativity are elements that align with the characteristics of this personality type.

Try it for yourself

Maybe you belong to this Type 7, if you recognize the following:

☐ Are you easily inspired by people and their experiences?

☐ Do you want to maintain a positive mood and is it easy for you to change the mood of others?

☐ Do you create a lot of opportunities for yourself and don't like to be stopped?

☐ Are you surprised, how some people find life difficult and problematic?

☐ When you have deep and painful emotions, can you easily find an explanation for them and therefore get rid of the pain?

☐ Is your favorite defense your charm and avoiding conflict by "talking through your teeth"?

☐ Do you have an exceptional ability to generate new ideas and concepts?

☐ Is your head full of ideas and plans?

Healthy Mode

Healthy Type 7s are typically "renaissance" people, who may be highly educated in a variety of areas. People of this style love adventure, have many talents and an amazing ability to enjoy the "taste" of life.

As a general rule, they evoke love with their special mix of charm and curiosity while being sociable, generous and seeking new horizons. Unlike Type 6s, who anticipate a negative future, Type 7s lean toward the positive and always anticipate what will happen next, filled with a sense of "hooray for tomorrow!"

Healthy Type 7s are great at enthusiastically accepting life's gifts, even the smallest ones. And often, highly conscientious Type Sevens are resilient and bounce back easily after troubles and losses.

At best, people of this type realistically accept the need for both a long-term commitment and the difficulties in their daily lives. By coming face to face and integrating the different dimensions of life's problems, Type 7s gain depth and are even more capable of experiencing true joy. Many of them say that the ability to make necessary sacrifices gives their lives a stable structure, within which they can find much variety.

Receptive to new experiences, healthy Type 7s also have a certain vulnerability when they treat the world completely helpless,

perceiving each day with principled openness.

Healthy Type 7s teach us by example how to enjoy life and celebrate every day. Their creeds are "doing everything with pleasure. " Even at their oldest age, they look and act young.

Passion Capital

The Gluttony. Wanting everything, he gets excited about everything and goes everywhere without delving into anything because he is immersed in hedonistic pleasures.

 ## State of Stress, Unhealthy Mode or Disintegration from 7 to 1

When Type 7 is under pressure and feels that their options are limited, they begin to display Type 1 behavior patterns. They can no longer perceive the entire situation and begin to pay attention to the details of some specific task. Type 7 gets angry easily and judges themselves more than others.

They pursue what they want and eventually lose control, flee from painful realities, and become impulsive and irresponsible.

 ## Security or Integration from 7 to 5

When Type 7 is resourceful and emotionally animated, they use Type 5 behaviors; becomes more introverted and reflective. It becomes more important for him to spend time collecting knowledge and spending time alone with a good book.

He does not like boredom and does any exciting activity that comes to mind. And yet, they don't feel satisfied enough.

 **Development and growth path for Type 7**

For Type 7, being "here and now", no matter what the moment, makes him develop a special ability and that is to perceive reality soberly. He faces and accepts negative situations such as pain and sadness without running away from them. If he does this, he will feel more grounded, happier, and more attractive.

The healthy Type 7 can step away from the topic and take a bird's eye view of things and organize them, so they can shape their thoughts and ideas. He must take responsibility for what you propose to do and see it through to the end. Type 7 likes to have many options to execute, but should try to focus on one and prioritize it until it is finished.

Vice

Gluttony is the feeling that there are an infinite number of possibilities in the world and the need to use them all. Insatiable hunger aims for something in the future that can satisfy the type 7.

 **How to communicate with a Type 7 person**

- When the area is nice, Type 7s can fully demonstrate their abilities.

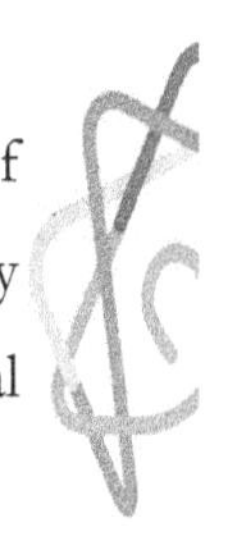

- They don't like situations where they have to take care of their superiors and subordinates, or scenarios where they have little freedom, so they try to build frank and equal relationships as much as possible.

Fixation

Planning is a way to avoid worry by distracting the mind. Constant mental activity, many things occupy the mind at the same time of Type 7.

Virtue

Common sense is the ability to stay in the present without disturbing expectations, emotions and thoughts.

Visual and Auditory Spatial Intelligence

Those of Type 7 are related to Visual and Auditory Intelligence whose ability is to perceive through images or sounds. The sense of sight develops before the knowledge of language, you learn to see the world before you can name it, you learn music before lyrics.

Most of the fundamental ideas about nature are essentially simple and as a general rule the sciences express them through understandable and memorable visual forms. On many occasions you recognize the image of something, place, object, person, even if you forget its name.

Keywords that symbolize Type 7

Optimistic, happy/cheerful, free, full of curiosity, rich in ideas, energetic/enthusiastic, stimulating, short-tempered, versatile, materialistic/appetizing, superficial and broad (boring), adventurous.

LEADER

Leader-Justice
Enneatype 8

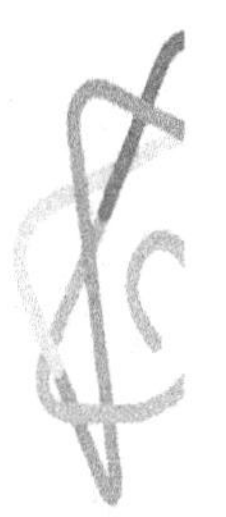

"For every house is builded by some man; but he that built all things is God."

Hebrews 3:4

King James Version

Type Eights are high-energy leaders and initiators of new ideas. Focused on their immediate needs and justice, they are energetic, self-confident, combative and destructive. They love to take responsibility, protect their friends and family.

Type 8s like to be in control of the situation and are relentless in making those who do wrong pay the consequences. They tend to be self-confident and trust their judgment, which puts them in the position of protectors of others.

Type 8 people have a big heart hidden under shining armor. They are willing to open their vulnerable side, which they usually protect, only if they feel someone's trust. They are extremely irritable and short-tempered. Excessive food, sex, alcohol and drugs: this takes them to extremes because they are attracted to the experience of "walking on the edge of the knife". Sometimes lust (the appetite to have everything "here and now") takes the form of a desire to control others completely. They blame the weakness of others and deny their own. Type Eights are fast-paced, trying to achieve intimacy through combat.

"Let them serve me."

THE I

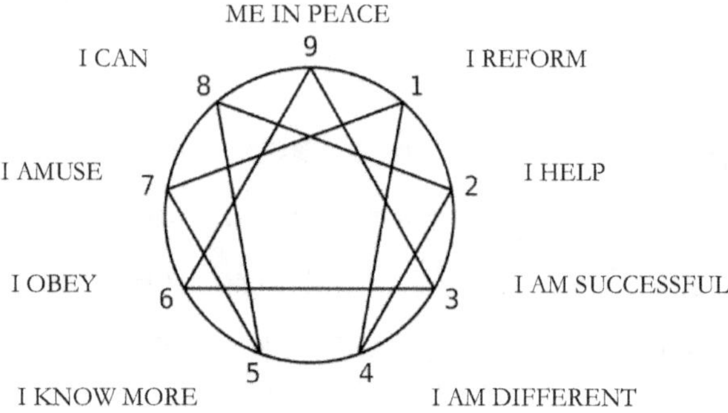

Type Eights are vital in taking up a lot of space, and especially need control over their personal space. Prone to dichotomous thinking, going from one extreme to another. They do not like to talk about their experiences and open their vulnerable soul only to close and reliable people.

"Don't let them stop me."

They are afraid of being vulnerable, so they constantly monitor the situation and reject anyone who limits them in something.

CHARACTERS FROM SERIES AND MOVIES

In the "Billions" series, Bobby Axelrod is portrayed as an 8W7.

Bobby is the type of person whose main goal in life is success. The passion for success goes hand in hand with the drive for status.

Bobby doesn't like to ask, but he doesn't want to give up anything and tries to get others to give him without having to ask openly. Since he was young, he sought to be financially independent, he does not monitor his bank account, he does not save, and he spends more than he has. "He is generous with other people's money and "greedier" with his own."

He is vengeful if he does not achieve his goal or is discovered or in his true intentions, while trying to maintain a good image; He says there will be a chance for cold revenge where it will all be worth it.

Manipulation of information, defamation and slander are common in this subtype. The strategic lies to discredit the other are so well concocted that he himself loses track of the boundary between reality and fiction.

Once a place of recognition has been achieved, the fight

continues, now seeking constant adaptation so as not to lose the privileges achieved. There can be no limit to trampling on anyone, or to construct lies that invalidate anyone who interferes in their path to the podium.

In the movie "Scarface", Tony Montana is a Type 8W7.

Photo taken from Netflix.

Tony is the opposite of someone cold and pragmatic. He does not ignore or repress his feelings. On the contrary, he has quite defined ethics and values, which are reflected in his most iconic phrases and in the actions that led to his eventual downfall. That's why he's so overprotective of his sister.

His obsession with her caused him to kill his best friend. There are two theories about this: Tony knew that Manny would make her suffer with infidelities, taking into account what a womanizer his friend was; and the other is that Tony was deeply in love with his sister. Either option would clearly reflect the nature of the actions towards her: strong sentimentality.

The scene in the restaurant also projects part of his feelings. Tony reproaches the rich who live in luxury and security because they don't know what it's like to get their hands dirty and work hard to be where they are.

He also does not tolerate being made to look foolish or made fun of. Maybe that's why he got angry when Manny was with his sister. After all, Tony warned him about it, so he might feel betrayed too.

> "I want what's coming for me. The world and everything in it."

> "The eyes, boy. They never lie."

These lines and the scene in which he ironically looks towards the airship that shines "The world is yours" with a tired and empty face as if he were under the post-madness clarity indicates where his destiny was going. He is dogmatic and does not even try to manipulate people's feelings.

He has moody behaviors and his one-sided affection for his family, along with his obsession with his sister and frequent outbursts of emotion, drag him down.

Tony has many silly moments where he jokes with the people around him (for example: intro interrogation scene, flirting with Elvira when buying the car, among others). He is extremely charismatic and even after all of his horrible crimes, he still comes across as funny and likeable. Alejandro Sosa, was furious for missing the crucial hit on the speech giver, and what did Tony say? "Okay, we'll do it next month."

He does not relate to others through a hardened and insensitive attitude, nor is he reasonably warm and friendly, presenting himself as a protector of a group or a controlling body thereof.

He acts purely through his personal intensity and charisma, taking on most of his interactions with his strength and magnetism. There is an undeniable theatrical aspect to the way he carries himself, and his amplified lustful quality, even by Type 8 standards, is reflected in how he immediately reacts to any situation he finds himself in, without grand strategies, but based purely on in his ability to improvise and overwhelm others in the moment.

Tony has a positive attitude that is purely his own, and we mostly see him acting of his own free will and behaving as if he believes he is the only one who can do it. His ultimate confidence in himself and his ability to behave purely through his Type 8, without needing anything or anyone, is reflected in his negotiations with Sosa, at which point he says "All I have in this world are my balls and my word; and I do not break them for anyone."

In the "Fast & Furious" series, Dominic Toretto is portrayed as an 8W9.

Photo taken from Universal Studios.

Toretto is the boss, the leader, the one who sets the rules and they are usually imposing and challenging. He protects his team, which he calls family, and can sacrifice himself for them.

It is visceral so it is recommended not to catch it the wrong way. He is scary because he is passionate and, in his quest, to establish power, he can be aggressive and antagonistic. Although it is difficult for him to show affection, much of what he does is to take care of his loved ones.

In the "Money Heist" series, Tokio is portrayed as an 8W7.

Photo taken from Netflix.

Tokyo is challenging, powerful, dominant, proud, intimidating, but also determined and protective of her people, especially Rio. This is an ideal personality type for leading teams.

"As in chess, there are times when to win it is necessary to sacrifice a piece. "

"If you think about it, it's never a good day for a robbery."

"At the end of the day, love is a good reason for all things to fail. "

"Things are going to get very ugly and I'm not one to sit still. I'm more of a shooter."

In the "The Lord of the Rings" series, Gimli is portrayed as an 8W7.

Gimli lacks logic and internal analytical system. Decisions are based precisely on your internal values that you formed over years; That is why his willingness to show that he is competitive and strong is very helpful to the community.

He takes actions based on the concrete and present situation, without involving others as much, as when he tries to destroy the ring after learning of its danger. Concerned more with internal identity than logic, he competes to prove himself to Legolas and his values of being a logic-overriding dwarf. He doesn't like feeling inferior when trying to keep up with Aragorn and Legolas, or showing his fear when walking the paths of the dead.

In the "Game of Thrones" series, Tywin Lannister is portrayed as an 8W9.

"The surnames are still alive. Only they live."

It is the law of life, to die one day. There is no personal glory or power left when you die. But only the last name remains. It's a line that makes you think about what's important and even makes you feel hopeful.

"A man who has to say 'I am the king' is not a real king."

This line remained a golden word from Tywin to the young king. No one will believe you have power if you just shout your title. Many times, we proclaim the position we hold and people laugh behind our backs.

"The lion doesn't care what the sheep think."

These words describe Tywin's arrogance very well. Like other prominent Lannisters, he considered himself superior to everyone else.

In the "Game of Thrones" series, Cersei Lannister is portrayed as an 8W9.

Photo taken from HBO.

"When it comes to fighting for the throne, you win or you die."

It means you need to be prepared when you do something big. There will be great turning points and events in our lives. Why don't you try to remember this phrase in those moments?

"I wanted to do something very good, very pure. Maybe I'm not a monster."

Cersei complained to Tyrion about the loss of her children. She did whatever it took to gain power, but in the end, she lost her most precious children. Sadness and regret permeate.

In the "Game of Thrones" series, Arya Stark is portrayed as an 8W7.

Photo taken from HBO

"I don't care if someone dies."
Arya tells Tywin that people say they won't kill Rob. Tywin then asked Arya if Rob believed the story and she looked him in the eyes and replied: I also feel uneasy about this situation. It feels like a prophecy that no one will be saved.

"Nothing is better or worse than anything else. Nothing is simply nothing."
Aria is a character who is surrounded by the fear of death. "My family died, and I was greeted with betrayal wherever I went."

Arya didn't say this line in a comforting way when she met the man who was slowly dying. Aria told him what it was like to die. It's a line that makes you think deeply about what death is.

ANALYSIS OF A BIBLICAL CHARACTER:

When exploring the biblical figure of Moses, we can discern traits that suggest he embodies the characteristics of Type 8 in the Enneagram.

Moses's Strength

One of the most notable traits of Type 8 is their innate strength and their desire to be a powerful leader. Moses, from his divine calling on Mount Sinai, demonstrates strong and decisive leadership. In Exodus 3:10, God instructs Moses: "Come now, therefore, and I will send thee unto Pharaoh, that thou mayest bring forth my people, the children of Israel."

Moses accepts this challenge without hesitation, reflecting his nature as a strong leader and protector of his people.

Passion for Justice and Protecting the Oppressed

Type 8 individuals are renowned for their passion for justice and their desire to protect the oppressed. Moses, in his role as the leader of the Israelites, displays deep concern for justice and the protection of his people. In Exodus 2:11-12, we read about Moses defending an oppressed Hebrew against an Egyptian: "And it came to pass in those days, when Moses was grown, that he went out unto his brethren, and looked on their burdens: and he spied an Egyptian smiting a Hebrew, one of his brethren. And he looked this way and that way, and when he saw that there was no man, he slew the Egyptian, and hid him in the sand."

This act by Moses reveals his passion for justice and his willingness to protect the oppressed, characteristic of Type 8.

Intensity and the Courage to Challenge Authority

Another distinctive aspect of Type 8 is their intensity and their courage to challenge authority when they deem it necessary. Moses, in his confrontation with the Egyptian pharaoh to secure the release of the Israelites, demonstrates this bravery and determination. In Exodus 5:1-2, Moses and Aaron stand before the pharaoh: "And afterward Moses and Aaron went in, and told Pharaoh, Thus saith the Lord God of Israel, Let my people go, that they may hold a feast unto me in the wilderness."

This bold declaration before Egypt's supreme ruler reflects Moses's courage and determination, characteristic of Type 8.

The Struggle for Control and Autonomy

Type 8 often grapples with the desire for control and autonomy. Moses, in various biblical passages, fights to maintain control and autonomy for the people of Israel as they journey through the wilderness en route to the Promised Land. His resistance to the complaints and disobedience of the people is evident in Numbers 20:10-12. In this passage, Moses strikes the rock to bring forth water, emphasizing his determination to exercise control and maintain autonomy. However, this action ultimately leads to consequences.

Moses, through his strength, passion for justice, courage to challenge authority, and struggle for control and autonomy, can be identified as an example of Type 8 in the Enneagram, "The Protector" or "The Challenger." His role as a strong leader and defender of the Israelites in their quest for freedom and justice reflects the characteristics of this personality type.

Try it for yourself

Maybe you belong to this Type 8, if you recognize the following:

☐ Do you feel enormous responsibility and sometimes have the feeling that the whole world rests on your shoulders?

☐ Is it important that you feel that you have control of your space and everything that belongs to you?

☐ Don't you show weakness and may feel contempt for people who don't really try to take control of their lives?

☐ Do you tend to see extremes in situations? Fair or unfair; a person is strong or weak. For you there is no middle ground.

☐ Do you like to delight in food and drink? Should any need you desire be met immediately?

☐ Do you make decisions quickly and are you able to take responsibility for yourself if no one else is around?

Healthy Mode

Healthy Type 8s are dynamic, strong-willed and independent.

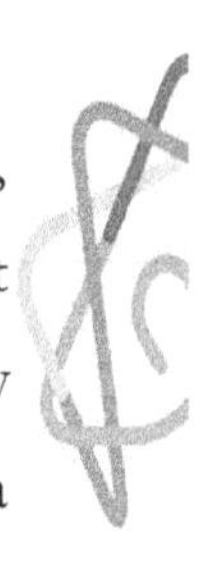

They are natural leaders who inspire others, protect the weak, and fight for justice. They are simple and try to get to the root of everything. In society, they take a pro-social position. They can boldly and decisively introduce new ideas that will have a significant positive effect on the environment. They are honest and show a thirst for life in all their affairs.

Healthy Type Eights are generous and loyal friends who protect the vulnerable areas of their loved ones. They show solidarity with the small, weak and defenseless. Protection often becomes the primary motivation for Type 8s to reform the system or organization.

And while this impulse is very sincere, it is also a metaphor for how Type 8s feel about themselves. After all, beneath their strong outer armor lives a tender young part, which they greatly appreciate inside. We can say that aggressive and vulnerable parts coexist within it at the same time, and in some way, they are connected to each other. And this young part of the 8 is innocent, open and capable of seeing the world, as if for the first time, with the frankness of a child.

David Shapiro comments: "Normal feelings are clouded by most of those people who are usually diagnosed as impulsive or psychopathic characters" (Type 8), as well as "some of those who are classified as passive neurotic characters or narcissistic characters. (Type 7)." (Shapiro: 1989).

A healthy Type 8 is very aware of what true strength is and also the difference from violence. He uses his power not to distance himself from people by building walls, but to draw closer to them through care and protection.

 **Passion Capital**

Lust. The excess of things, positions, power, has its origin in childhood and personality. Tony Montana in the movie Scarface after the midpoint of the movie, arrives at the bank with bags of money that increase day by day making the banker worried about the excess money.

State of Stress, Unhealthy Mode or Disintegration from 8 to 5

When Type 8 is under pressure or feels like they have "bitten off more than they can chew," they begin to exhibit Type 5 behavior patterns: withdrawing from others, considering new ways of acting, and not involving them in their problems. and personal sorrows. He becomes a ruthless dictator and sees those who disagree with him as traitors and enemies.

 **Security or Integration from 8 to 2**

When the Leader is safe and can "put his arms down," he begins to display Type 2 behavior patterns and pays more attention to the needs of other people. Then he is very courteous, takes good care of his loved ones and those in need. Confident and decisive. He becomes a great leader who fights for the people.

 **Development and growth path for Type 8**

You must build a connection with the vulnerable inner side, where there are "soft" emotions and develop the ability to simply be in the present, without trying to influence the situation, take control or responsibility.

If you feel angry, take a deep breath and wait 7 seconds. Listen carefully to what the other person has to say, respect their values that differ from yours, accepting them as they are, even if they are sometimes ambiguous.

Admit your weaknesses to be truly strong. Savor and accept negative emotions without running away from them. By being kind to others, you become accommodating, more open and loving, like a healthy Two.

Vice

Lust is a strong need to seize and possess. What Type 8 seeks to capture can vary: strength - control - people - power - food.

 **How to communicate with a Type 8 person**

- If you get emotional, Type 8 people will get emotional too; so, don't be so expressive and tell him calmly.

- Showing that you understand him is a sign that you trust him, so show him deep understanding and try to accompany him.

- If a Type 8 person is your subordinate, they set big goals rooted in what they really want to do, and supporting them will give them great power.

Fixation

Justice is the feeling that the responsibility of the world falls on your shoulders. This commitment has no limits and you must constantly fight for what you want to achieve.

Virtue

Innocence is the feeling that everything is in balance and no one is to blame for anything.

Basic Intelligence

Those of Type 8 are related to Basic Intelligence and is what is produced to satisfy the permanent and general intelligence requirements of the organization in question. It is used above all to respond to the information needs that arise during the production of strategic intelligence and prospective or estimative intelligence. Therefore, it is prepared taking into account the strategic objectives of the organization. Since it becomes an important store of intelligence, it is also used to meet information demands during the production of tactical, operational and operational intelligence.

Keywords that symbolize Type 8

Challenging and powerful difficulties, power of action, intensity, control, dominant, strong-willed, black and white, intimidating, self-confidence, authoritarian power.

THE PEACEMAKER

Mediator-Peacemaker
Enneatype 9

"For thou hast possessed my reins: thou hast covered me in my mother's womb. I will praise thee; for I am fearfully and wonderfully made: marvellous are thy works; and that my soul knoweth right well".

Psalm 139: 13-14

King James Version

Type Nines appreciate peace and harmony. They are peaceful, passive, balanced, gentle, affectionate, negligent and sleep well literally and figuratively. Exceptionally intuitive, the type nine dreams of an ideal spouse because an alliance with a lover is extremely important.

At their core, Type 9s are motivated by love and therefore perceive themselves as a tool for achieving overall well-being. Unlike Type 2, who loves individuals, Type 9's love is more general and encompasses many people at once.

They are diplomats and humanitarians which makes them

excellent at resolving conflicts. Because they intuitively strive for peace, harmony, and unity, it is easy for them to find points of connection between their opponents' sides. Type 9s can patiently build a win-win solution by taking small, positive steps. They are able to express the hard, uncomfortable truth in a way that other people don't feel the need to defend themselves. They are practical and pragmatic. They can defend themselves in any "battle."

I AM NOT... HOW TO BE...

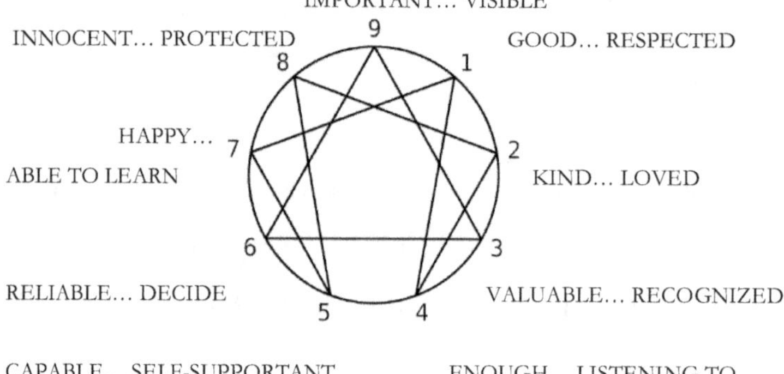

Type 9 people tend to flee from conflict and generally show a passive attitude. They prefer to focus their actions on consensus and avoid stridency in their behavior. Furthermore, they let others make important decisions.

Socially and in groups, Type 9s may seem like good listeners, but they often wander in and out of conversations. They are good peacemakers, counselors who support family and friends. They

find it difficult to defend themselves by saying no. Type Nines find it difficult to make decisions and set priorities. They avoid conflict and sweep problems under the rug. Finishing any project and setting goals is difficult for them, because they get distracted and entertained by things that are of little importance.

"Don't pressure me."

Type Nines tend to merge with others and prevent them from feeling empty. Time alone is important as it allows them to reconnect with themselves. They oscillate between obsequiousness and complete disdain, and can be very stubborn. By blaming others and external circumstances, they often refuse to take responsibility for themselves. They repel people who disturb their peace. However, to avoid a confrontation, they may obey each other's wishes.

They accept situations deeply, are emotionally stable and calm without appearing cold. They use empathy as a weapon to unite groups in harmony.

 **CHARACTERS FROM SERIES AND MOVIES**
In the movie "Scarface", Elvira Hancock is a Type 9W8.

Elvira is sarcastic and likes to make connections between things. She does and says what she feels; she is fed up with everything. Elvira never feels or thinks anything deeply and subordinates herself to her surroundings. She is elusive, impatient and

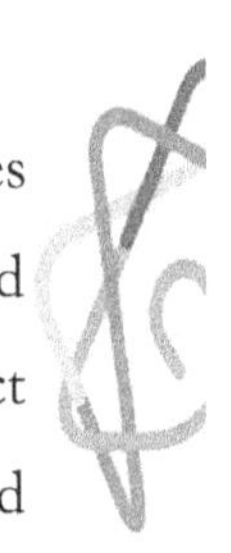

arrogant.

"We are not winners, we are losers. " "Can't you see what we've become?"

Elvira represents the unhealthy self-preservation of Type 9. All about meeting her physical needs to find solace, in her case through drugs and liquor. She flits around the house all day trying to numb the pain of life. Elvira has an 8 Wing due to her direct and aggressive streak, especially when Tony is trying to win her over.

In the "Fast & Furious" series, Han Lue is portrayed as a 9W1.

Photo taken from Universal Studios.

Han is creative and gentle, but also has a strong sense of morality and integrity. He fears being seen as bad or evil, and often strives to be the best person he can be. He has a strong sense of aesthetics and enjoys beauty in all its forms: cars and girls.

He cares deeply about the others on the team. He is compassionate and often puts the team's needs before his own. He is reserved by nature; he does not seek attention or be the life of the party. He prefers to stay in the background and let his actions speak for themselves. He is quiet and often prefers to spend time alone or with a small group of close friends. He is not comfortable being the center of attention and is sometimes introverted.

In the "The Simpsons" series, Homer Simpson is portrayed as a 9W8.

Foto tomada de Fox

Homer is unconscious and carefree, enjoying the moment instead of worrying about what others around him think and feel. When Homer eats a donut, he only thinks about how it smells, tastes, and feels at the moment. He doesn't think about past tastes, sights, smells, or sounds that are related to the donut he is eating. Homer is by no means unfriendly; On the contrary, his lively capacity for enjoyment makes him very good company; He is usually a happy and sometimes refined guy. In the first case, the great problems of life depend on a good or indifferent dinner; In the second, everything is a matter of good taste. Once an object has given you a feeling, there is nothing more to say or do about it.

When you look past his eccentricities and wacky personality, Homer is actually cognitively in tune with the emotional order, first and foremost, that makes him unique. He is always looking for new experiences to reinforce his sense of harmony. Homer is highly motivated to always stick to small routines like sitting in front of the TV, watching when Lisa or Bart wants to try something new, like different food for dinner.

No matter what may be happening, if something is presented to him that piques his interest, that is immediately what fills his entire brain.

In the "Outlander" series, Jamie Fraser is portrayed as a 9W8.

At first, he is unaware of his sister's feelings. He acted like an idiot, he didn't apologize. Then when Claire called him, he acted like a jerk to her too. He later realizes that he cares about other people's feelings and smooths things over.

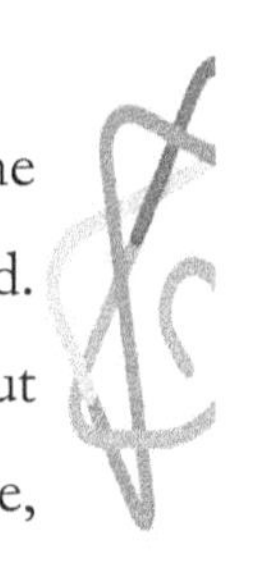

A prime example was the scene with the guy hitting his son, he tackled it head on...instead of working more subtly...and failed. The same with fixing the mill, he went to do it himself without taking other factors into account. So, when he gets into trouble, he improvises and it works out for him.

He seeks to help, save, protect, and sacrifice (i.e., receiving a beating by Laoghaire, his willingness to receive a flogging to protect Jenny's honor, his sympathy and leniency with his tenants simply because he knew they were having a difficult year).

What irritates him is not injustice based on his own moral code, but how it affects those around him (his anger at the clock burning the hay in Lollybrach). He is also very persuasive in terms of achieving harmony when he wants and uses very cat-like techniques to achieve it (convincing Claire to leave the baby in the woods, convincing Colum to reconcile with Dougal and return the extra money to him).

When he sent Claire to the future, he acted pragmatically because he knew that even if they both felt terrible about never seeing each other again, at least Claire and her baby would survive.

He is a realistic man, and on many occasions, he does not hesitate to say things as they are and according to what makes sense to him in a controlled and non-accentuated way. It seems that he cares about harmony, but he is only interested when his close people are involved, not at any other time.

In the "Star Wars" series, Padmé Amidala is portrayed as a 9W1.

"To be angry is to be human."

Padmé gave Anakin this quote, which is probably the cornerstone of the "Star Wars" series, which fights against the dark side of humans.

"So, this is how freedom dies, with thunderous applause."

It is a quote that expresses Padmé's despair at seeing Palpatine, who dismantled the Republic and became the first emperor of the Galactic Empire.

In the "Harry Potter" series, Harry Potter is portrayed as a 9W8.

Harry's internal sense of right and wrong serves to reinforce his choices; for example, when Remus Lupine abandons his family, Harry attacks him and calls him a coward. If you decide you don't want to be friends with someone, you won't force yourself to do so. No amount of trying will make him trust a teacher if he no longer does.

He has a tendency to suppress his strong emotions until he explodes with rage. Rejecting Draco Malfoy's offer of friendship, thwarting Dolores Umbridge's attempts to silence him regarding Voldemort's return, and identifying with his like-minded "uncle," Sirius Black, are all examples of how Harry responds to people who want to exert control. about him.

The only thing Harry likes more than taking on a new challenge is playing Quidditch. Much to Hermione's dismay, he frequently expresses a desire to spend time outdoors doing things instead of being cooped up in his room studying. He acts quickly and impulsively, whether playing with the Marauder's Map or trying to escape the Dursley house.

His blind spot is that he lives so much in the now, that he forgets to think about the sequence of events and how they might unfold. As an illustration, he was convinced that Draco had joined the Death Eaters long before anyone else. His unfavorable view of Snape diminishes greatly when he learns the truth; He finds it difficult to rescind his only conclusions and becomes enraged when forced to reevaluate Dumbledore's actions and goals.

Harry tends to act hastily, to solve problems without considering the possible inconveniences or consequences. When under pressure, he can be rude, aggressive and disobedient.

Most of Harry's childhood was spent locked in a closet, where he endured abusive treatment from his aunt, uncle, and cousin because he had no other choice and had become accustomed to their treatment. You often lack the drive to make positive changes in your life and do not care about your academic performance. Things that make Harry anxious, or that he doesn't want to do or aren't good at, are often postponed until later, causing Harry to have to improvise at the last minute.

Harry does everything he can to avoid Hermione and Ron's constant fighting. His 8 Wing instincts are on full display in the moments he exploded at his great-aunt, dared Dudley to come after him after his godfather died, and attempted to confront Snape outside of class after overhearing him make a snarky comment about Hermione.

He sees her refusal to reveal Umbridge's sentence as a power play on her part. He becomes enraged and destroys Dumbledore's office. He loses his cool with his friends and suddenly wants everything to be okay again. When he's under pressure, his anxiety levels rise, at which point he starts to worry that everything is going to go wrong because of him, that Sirius is in danger, and that he can't think clearly.

He was raised by a very poor family in a very socialist society, however, he values freedom and rejects authority. He doesn't like government and has no respect for bureaucracy.

In the "Yo soy, Betty la Fea" series, Nicolás Mora is portrayed as a 9W1.

Photo taken from the RCN Channel

Nicolás provides emotional support to Betty, he falls in love with Patricia after barely knowing her and avoids conflict, although he has problems setting his limits, such as when he is invited to a party just to use him and make fun of him.

He was never seen to have motivations to know, investigate, or fear of feeling useless or not knowing enough. When he generated some type of conflict it was more because he did not know how to act socially.

He helped Betty or made certain excuses for her with Don Hermes to avoid conflicts. He broke up with Patricia for avoiding a major conflict with Betty. In one of the episodes, he gives the phone to a girl he doesn't even know, although he doesn't agree because he wants to keep some peace.

When he was seen on the defensive it was very strange (like when he hit Germán or Don Armando) it was because they were bothering Betty. Type 9s can be very passive, but when their values are interfered with, they become defensive.

In the "The Lord of the Rings" series, Legolas is portrayed as a 9W8.

Photo taken from New Line Cinema

Legolas makes decisions based on instinct, he likes to feel in control, particularly of his physical environment because freedom and independence are important.

Legolas is supportive of the group, accepts the rules, and is pleasant. It focuses on maintaining harmony in its habitat. He

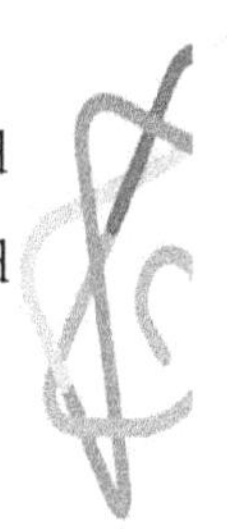

maintains a calm demeanor that others find relaxing. He joked with Gimli and maintained his dedicated code of honor and friendship with Aragorn.

The relationship with Gimli is actually a big deal because it's a symbolic friendship that speaks to healing the rift between elves and dwarves. Legolas and Gimli start out prejudiced against each other, but become great friends. He shows his loyalty here when he defends Gimli from Eomer's threat.

"You would die before your stroke fell."

Legolas also has a close friendship with Aragorn. Being loyal to his friend, he utters this phrase in the face of a battle that is difficult to win:

"Your Friends Are with You, Aragorn."

As Legolas looked at Mordor from Rohan, he predicted a catastrophic event with a poetic expression:

"The Stars Are Veiled. Something Stirs in The East. A Sleepless Malice. The Eye of The Enemy Is Moving. He is Here."

Gimli mentions that he never believed that his end would be fighting alongside an elf. The friendship between the two of them is used in books and movies to make us laugh. Legolas answers him with a question and a smile on his face:

"What About [Dying] Side by Side with A Friend?"

ANALYSIS OF A BIBLICAL CHARACTER:

When we delve into the biblical figure of Job, we can discern many traits aligning with Type 9 in the Enneagram.

The Quest for Peace and Harmony

One of the most pronounced attributes of Type 9 is an enduring yearning for peace and harmony. Job, throughout his life and writings, displays a profound longing for peace and reconciliation. In Job 9:17 (King James Version), Job expresses his desire to find peace with God: "For he breaketh me with a tempest, and multiplieth my wounds without cause."

Despite facing countless trials and tribulations, Job pursues peace and reconciliation, characteristic of Type 9.

The Tendency to Avoid Conflict

Type 9 individuals innately shy away from conflicts and confrontations. Job, on multiple occasions, demonstrates this inclination by striving to maintain peace in his relationships and circumvent disputes. In Job 1:5 (King James Version), we learn about Job's efforts to preserve harmony within his family:

"And it was so, when the days of their feasting were gone

about, that Job sent and sanctified them, and rose up early in the morning, and offered burnt offerings according to the number of them all: for Job said, It may be that my sons have sinned, and cursed God in their hearts. Thus did Job continually."

Job endeavors to avoid conflicts among his children and God, exemplifying the peace-loving nature of Type 9.

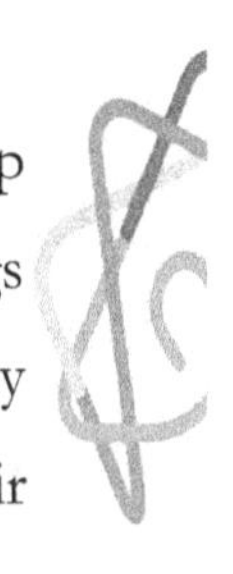

The Tendency to Neglect One's Own Needs

Type 9 individuals often tend to neglect their own needs in the pursuit of peace and harmony in their relationships. Job, throughout his sufferings, manifests this inclination by focusing on the problems of others and seeking God's will rather than addressing his own needs. In Job 42:3-6 (King James Version), Job humbles himself before God: "Who is he that hideth counsel without knowledge? Therefore, have I uttered that I understood not; things too wonderful for me, which I knew not. Hear, I beseech thee, and I will speak: I will demand of thee, and declare thou unto me. I have heard of thee by the hearing of the ear: but now mine eye seeth thee. Wherefore, I abhor myself, and repent in dust and ashes."

Despite experiencing profound suffering, Job's focus on peace and understanding is typical of Type 9, which often relegates its own needs.

The Pursuit of Unity and Reconciliation

Type 9 individuals highly value unity and reconciliation.

> Throughout his story, Job seeks reconciliation with God and endeavors to comprehend His will. In Job 42:10 (King James Version), we witness a transformation in his circumstances: "And the Lord turned the captivity of Job, when he prayed for his friends: also, the Lord gave Job twice as much as he had before."

This passage illustrates how, through prayer and reconciliation with his friends, Job finds peace and restoration, emblematic of Type 9.

Job, through his unceasing pursuit of peace and harmony, his inclination to avoid conflicts, his disregard for his own needs, his yearning for unity and reconciliation, and his focus on peace rather than confrontation, can be identified as an exemplar of Type 9 in the Enneagram, "The Peacemaker." His narrative and writings allow us to appreciate his profound desire to maintain peace and harmony amid trials and tribulations, reflecting the characteristics of this personality type.

Try it for yourself

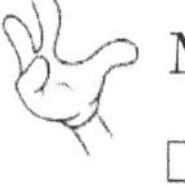

Maybe you belong to this Type 9, if you recognize the following:

☐ Are you trying to avoid conflict and find it difficult to say clearly that you don't want to do something?

☐ Can you easily see all points of view and factor them into your decision?

☐ Do you have a lot of time: "There is still a lot of time, I will wait until tomorrow"?

☐ Is it easier for you to determine what you don't want than what you do want?

☐ Do you easily neglect your needs in favor of someone else's?

☐ Do you often feel that you practically merge with other people, music, and nature?

☐ Do you have the ability to provide support and are you attentive to what is important to other people?

☐ Do you charge your "batteries" by being alone, but at the same time rely on the praise of others?

☐ Do you sometimes perceive that you are not noticed, but at the same time you feel better than others?

Healthy Mode

Healthy Type 9s are balanced, stable, unpretentious, tolerant, and find comfort in the company of another person. These are friends who always forgive and do not take offense. They are quite cheerful (like type 7), but they live mainly in the present, not the future.

Sometimes in the Enneagram, Type Nines are described as "ordinary people." At healthy levels of development, they are deeply humble and strive for an elegant simplicity in all their manners. Sometimes it even seems to them that other people simply will not remember them when they meet.

Healthy Type 9s have a gentle dynamism, a deep sense of self and their mission in life. Most of them try to help the world in a way that benefits everyone around them. A Type Nine describes this feeling like this: "When my department is successful at work, I feel successful too. My ego doesn't need anything. And as long as we're successful, I'm happy."

Passion Capital

Laziness. Which is equal to negligence, "I have sinned in thought, deed and omission." In order to carry out the party in peace, he lets terrible things happen by not putting a stop to it.

 ## State of Stress, Unhealthy Mode or Disintegration from 9 to 6

When the Mediator is under pressure, they begin to use Type 6 behavior patterns and become more skeptical about the motives of others. He finds it difficult to trust his own judgment and analyzes the situation over and over again. He becomes lazy and lethargic in everything, disconnects from all problems and conflicts, does not deal with problems and becomes negligent.

 ## Security or Integration from 9 to 3

When Type 9 feels safe and in harmony, they exhibit Type 3 behavior patterns. The Mediator focuses on the task at hand, what needs to be done, and important goals. He becomes very productive and loses his sense of proportion.

 ## Development and growth path for Type 9

You must develop the ability to act in this moment, and you also need to develop the ability to communicate clearly with others, even if this may lead to conflict.

Use your ability to adapt to the environment by interacting with role models and changing your environment. Speak consciously, knowing that not speaking will end in big trouble. Recognize that you are a great existence, not an insignificant existence, and take care of yourself. By prioritizing and acting like a healthy Type 3, you can be proud of your accomplishments.

Vice

Laziness is an inner need to do nothing, to rest, to wait and see what happens.

How to communicate with a Type 9 person

- Type 9 doesn't seem to insist on anything and doesn't want his rhythm to be disturbed, so he listens carefully to what he thinks.

- Sometimes they are not good at prioritizing, so try to get back to the objectives.

- Since they have a high level of agreeableness, when you want to improve the performance of people with Type 9, you should also try to be assertive.

Fixation

Procrastination is the desire to be calm and detached to avoid conflict. An attempt to create and maintain a sense of peace in every possible way, always and everywhere.

Virtue

Energy: When you let yourself be carried away by instinct, it manifests itself in spontaneous instinctive actions, not suppressed by thoughts or emotions.

Pattern Intelligence

Those of Type 9 are related to Pattern Intelligence. The pattern that is the organization of energy in the brain has a stabilizing or harmonizing function from which it could be assumed that resistance to change originates.

Keywords that symbolize Type 9

Peace/Tranquility, Empathy, Acceptance, Adaptation, Passivity, Stubbornness, Healing, Routines, Relaxation, Adaptation to environment, Being honest, not good at prioritizing.

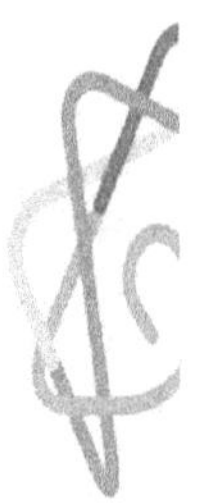

APPENDIX I

HR for Companies and producers

The enneagram is an effective system of personal growth and is applied in various fields, such as business, education, and counseling, beyond the world of psychology.

 **Are you concerned about building a highly productive team?**

Create highly productive teams, centralizing human resources information and visualizing skills. Using the content of this book you will be able to:

- Understand the characteristics of employees with the Enneagram.

- Resolve conflicts: providing clues about the different ways of understanding situations depending on personality.

- Centrally manage human resources information and skills for optimal placement.

- Simulate the location of collaborators using an organization chart.

- Reduce work stress and create healthy environments: because a person who knows himself will have more resources to face the challenges that our work poses, knowing where our limits and those of others are. As well as forms of self-regulation and self-control.

- Activate communication with self-disclosure of your profile.

- Distribute tasks and organize teams: optimizing the workforce by assigning tasks that are more in line with each person's way of being.

- View the proportion of men and women and the graduate rate in graphs.

- Do personnel selection processes: it helps you choose the right person for the right position.

- Improve communication within the company and with clients: knowing which perceptual channels of each individual are most effective to transmit our message.

INTEGRITY

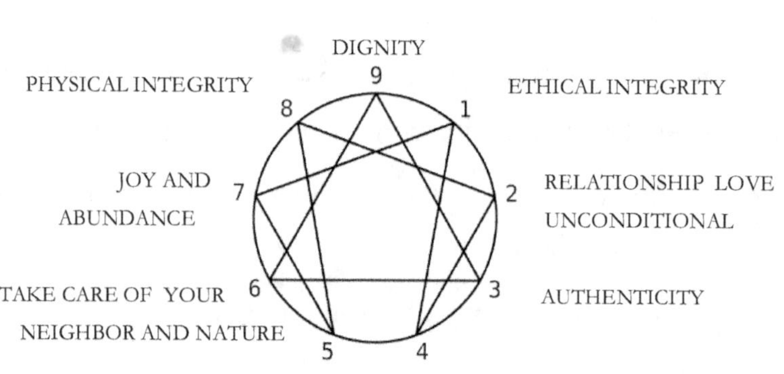

Use for team building.

Find out and share the group's types so that team members can learn about each other's personality traits. By getting to know each other's personalities, which you only knew on the surface, you will be able to deepen your relationship of trust.

Get to know the personalities of your subordinates

By knowing the types of subordinates, you will be able to visualize where they are good with their values and where they are weak with their defects. This will make it easier to manage the results because it will be clear how to teach.

Know your boss

On the other hand, by knowing the type of boss, subordinates can learn effective monitoring skills, such as when to ask for advice.

Know your type of organization

Additionally, if you collect the types of all employees, you can see the trend of the type as a company. If you aggregate by department, you can see the department type trend. If you know the type trend of the organization, it should be clear what type of human resources it can acquire in the future. In recent years, attention has focused on incorporating psychology into organizational management. What is the background behind this?

Psychology is common sense in organizational management

Years ago, production was mass; The central management method consisted of managers managing the development process of each line. However, in modern times, knowledge work, such as planning and design, is focused instead on manufacturing. In knowledge work, relationships affect productivity.

In recent years, Google has proven that psychological safety is essential to building highly productive teams. Organizational management has gone from managing work processes to managing human relationships. Therefore, psychology is becoming commonplace in companies.

Personality and talent management test

Personality testing has long been conducted in the form of assessments, primarily for the development of next-generation leaders. If a potentially malicious leader becomes president, it can have a negative impact on company performance. To avoid such human risks, it is common practice to use personality tests in talent management.

What measures are necessary to highlight the potential of employees?

By visualizing employee characteristics, you can understand the strategies that suit each individual.

You can complete the above with the following information:

Type 1 is someone who always fights for his ideals.

A person from the Type 1 team commented:

"We not only strive for improvement, but we also fight for equity and justice. We get angry and blame ourselves when we don't get the results we want. Furthermore, we feel impatient, no matter how much time I have, it is not enough."

However, because they hide their emotions such as anger in their hearts, they appear calm and collected to those around them.

"We treat people with honesty, openness and fairness, and we strive to keep our feet on the ground and strive for a better life."

Type 2 is kind and considerate.

Another Type 2 member said:

"We can't help but reach out to those who need it."

However, they become depressed when they discover that their kindness is not needed and angry when they are not appreciated. There is also a tendency to sacrifice one's own desires to seek good feelings for themselves.

I believe that the most important thing in human relationships is good communication and mutual understanding. They want to give love to others and expect them to give them love in return.

Type 3s act with goals and objectives in everything they do.
"We will do whatever it takes to achieve our goals and achieve success. All events can be executed efficiently while making effective use of time."

Additionally, instead of progressing on your own, as an excellent leader, you can move the organization and move toward its goals.

"Ultimately, we will let our potential flourish and actively go out into the world."

On the other hand, they have an extreme fear of failure and tend to avoid doing things that have no prospect of success.

Type 4 is an art lover.
"I value unique, creative and inspiring things, and I despise mediocrity and being equal to others."

Because they are very sensitive, they are affected by the personalities, moods, and subtleties of other people's minds. They are individualistic, honest and inquisitive who do not like to join large groups.

"I try to express my emotions in an artistic way."
On the other hand, they feel that they are not understood by

others and tend to have feelings of jealousy and envy.

Type 5 is a type of investigator.

"I collect data, reflect and act prudently. I think thinking and compiling information is the most important thing when it comes to acting."

Even though they are well informed, they do not share their knowledge with the world. They are often silent and on the sidelines.

"When you become an expert, you are willing to accumulate knowledge at the expense of others and create value with original ideas. However, I don't care about anything other than what interests me."

Type 6s are people who have a strong desire to maintain good relationships with those around them.

"That's why we focus on being honest, sincere and loyal."

They work hard because of their strong sense of responsibility and have a very strong emotional side. However, they are so afraid of making mistakes that they respect the rules and tend to rely on aspects outside of themselves. They avoid solving on their own and delay making decisions.

Type 7s focus on having fun in life.

"I take on challenges and enjoy life, as it is full of possibilities and diversity."

Bright, cheerful and frank, you tend to make plans for the future and pursue your dreams.

" I hate situations that restrict me and I want to share my happy life with others."

It is possible for him to act brilliantly even in serious situations and adversity.

Type 8s are very assertive.

Aim to be the first person, trust in your own power and push things forward without depending on others. Overflowing with confidence.

"I like to move people and influence those around me, and try to help people without refusing when they ask me."

However, they have strong likes and dislikes, and tend to completely eliminate people who are aggressive towards them.

Type 9s are stable and calm people.

"I am very calm and calm from the inside out."

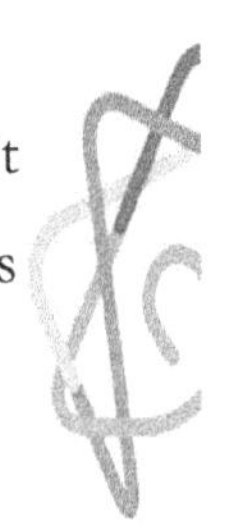

If such a situation exists, you tend to be a determined person. It is important for them to maintain a peaceful and harmonious daily life.

However, when situations happen, they have great creative power based on their imagination and vision. It makes the environment calmer, there are no emotional ups and downs and they can build relationships peacefully. Therefore, they are not suitable for launching new products or changing procedures.

Instinct Center Group Personality Test (Type 1, Type 8, Type 9)

They tend to rely on intuition and bodily sensations to make decisions. Even if a conclusion is reached through logical thinking, instinctive senses and real feelings are emphasized in the end.

Therefore, although they have a hard time finding arguments to persuade others, they tend to be stubborn. In the three Types of this group, likes and dislikes based on real feelings clearly emerge.

Emotional and personality traits to take into account.

Instinct-focused personality types tend to focus more on present sensations than on the past or future. They are people capable of surrendering to their bodily sensations and instincts, and fully enjoying the happiness they feel in the present moment.

However, on the other hand, in an unstable environment, it is easy to be misled by feelings of tension and impatience. In particular, attention should be paid to the emotion of "anger."

 **Emotional Center Group Personality Test (Type 2, Type 3, Type 4)**

Types 2, 3, and 4 tend to emphasize the evaluation of others and often worry about how people see them. Additionally, they want to express an established self-image to attract the attention of bosses.

Self-identity is generally formed based on past experiences:

- Type 2: What have you done to others?
- Type 3: What have you achieved?
- Type 4: What is the action that makes you feel like yourself?

Emotional and personality traits to take into account.

They form their identity based on their perception of themselves, but since people's senses are constantly changing and easily worn down, Types 2, 3, and 4 are likely to have difficulty stabilizing their self-image.

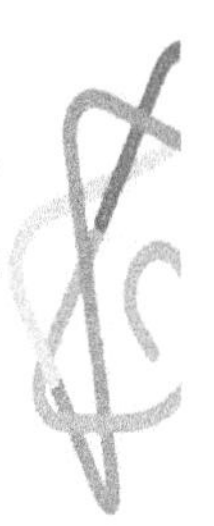

Shame is also an emotion that can easily become a problem. When there is a discrepancy between self-image and reality, it is easy to feel shame and guilt.

Thinking Center Personality Test (Type 5, Type 6, Type 7).

Those in this group can accurately draw a vision of the future based on predictions from the analysis of the current situation. They are good at gathering information and have observation skills. They look for an environment conducive to their thoughts, preferring stillness and inner peace. They have an affinity for abstract concepts and logical thinking.

They tend to use their natural planning abilities to deal with anxiety about the future. Therefore, there are many people who are too biased.

Emotional and personality traits to take into account.

They can come up with many ideas, but they have a hard time classifying them. They often have problems with their ability to make decisions.

They are also inclined to be dominated by the feeling of "anxiety" and tend to make big and small plans to alleviate the distress.

Enneagram: self-analysis and work aptitude test.

Using the Enneagram promotes self-understanding and understanding of others and, along with personal growth, it is possible to make great positive changes.

The Enneagram is also a catalyst for self-acceptance and the acceptance of others. Modern society has become more mind-oriented.

Knowing your Aptitude with the Enneagram.

The Enneagram is also useful for understanding an employee's compatibility with their job, that is, how well the employee's personality fits the job. However, it's not as simple as the Enneagram automatically finding matching jobs for individual employees. Even if you think a contributor is good for a role, it may not be the right job for that person.

By using the Enneagram, you can objectively understand your aptitude without being bound by your own stereotypes and images. It may be more appropriate to say that "understanding aptitude" using the Enneagram is harnessing individual characteristics when objectively viewing and understanding general tendencies.

The effect of the Enneagram on human resource management.

The Enneagram is a tool to know yourself and understand others. Through self-understanding and acceptance of others, employees develop self-confidence, adaptability, and communication skills. These qualities will give employees the independence to think and act for themselves.

Self-motivation is an essential quality in any profession or job.

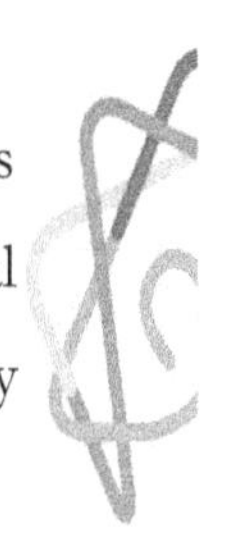

Additionally, the Enneagram allows for management that takes advantage of employee characteristics, creating mutual understanding between workers and a greater sense of stability within the organization.

Fluid relationships in the workplace facilitate the functioning of the organization, which will also increase the capacity, vitality of the team and the organization to get ahead on projects.

Use of human resources through personality diagnosis.

Human beings are influenced by the environment in which they grow up. However, no matter how much it affects you, you will not change the temperament you were born with.

That nature is a person's talent of being. To create a management system that considers and uses each temperament, a system like the Enneagram that objectively and concretely explains the differences in that talent will be essential.

Effects on labor relations.

As I have already said, the Enneagram helps us better understand others. It allows us to learn about different values and worldviews, avoiding misunderstandings and conflicts in advance to facilitate the construction of human relationships. Even if the other person is under stress, you can bring out their potential by deepening your understanding.

Additionally, the Enneagram can be used for group and organizational activities. Understanding the personality types of each member of your group allows you to take advantage of their diverse and versatile personalities. This will increase the group's potential and focus on achieving its goals.

Explanation of leadership styles by personality type.

If all employees demonstrate their own leadership style rather than an ideal leadership style, powerful work with presence is possible.

I will present to you the differences in leadership for each of the nine personality types, so you can recognize the characteristics of each one and try to practice management that makes the best use of the positive parts:

Type 1: Reformer
(Trying to be right)

1.   He has a strong sense of responsibility, is serious and trustworthy, so people believe in him.

2.   You have high standards and think: "I should."

3.   Good at quality control.

4.   You tend to be serious and stubborn because you are convinced of your own opinion, so be careful.

5.   Responds flexibly to the environment and maintains a positive atmosphere.

Type 2: Helper

(People who want to help others)

1.   Is considerate, encouraging and supportive, taking into account the feelings of others. Strengthens ties in the workplace and creates a good environment.

2.   Good at praising and improving the positive points of subordinates.

3.   Lack of ability to think strategically or systematically.

4.   You may feel overwhelmed by your emotions or get too involved in the other person's territory.

Type 3: Achiever

(People who pursue success)

1.   They have a strong desire to improve, and believe they can do it if they try.

2.   They increase motivation towards objectives and bring out the potential of subordinates.

3.   They focus on having a method that carefully understands not only the goal but also the process and the feelings of those around them.

4.   They change policies and methods flexibly, but explain enough so that people around them do not feel uncomfortable.

5.   They are careful not to deviate from their politics by trying to curry favor with those around them.

Type 4: Single person

(Person who tries to be special))

1. Has a developed sense of beauty and rich sensitivity.

2. He can think of ideas from a different angle than other people.

3. Is able to interact in a way that respects the feelings of others.

4. At first glance, he gives the impression that he is unapproachable, so it is good to show a humorous side to the environment.

5. He tries to be as stable and consistent as possible, since mood swings tend to affect subordinates.

Type 5: Investigator
(Person who acquires knowledge and observes)

1. He is smart and technically savvy.

2. He has the ability to take a step back, exercise his observation eyes and analyze without getting caught in the whirlpool.

3. Able to generate innovative ideas without being bound by preconceived notions.

4. He likes to think and come to conclusions on his own, but he needs to share his progress with the people around him and his peers.

Type 6: Loyal

(Safe and prudent)

1.   They are serious workers who can manage the movement of resources such as people, goods and money in a balanced manner as a generalist.

2.   Able to detect potential problems early.

3.   They have a tendency for their sense of role as boss to become too strong.

4.   They must be careful not to overprotect their subordinates by spending too much time guiding them or providing too detailed guidance.

5.   They must control anxiety and anger.

6.   They need to relate to subordinates with a feeling of stability as if they had their feet on the ground.

Type 7: Enthusiastic
(Planner looking for fun)

1.   He is a mood creator, friendly, fun and brightens the atmosphere at work.

2.   Full of ideas, think and act immediately.

3.   While he is optimistic about things, be careful because he may cover up or overlook problems.

4.   Sometimes he is so caught up in his own story that he doesn't listen to what others have to say.

Type 8: Challenger
(Person seeking strength and affirmation)

1.   Powerful, hungry, frank and confident.

2.   Strong and decisive character.

3.   People around him think: "If you leave it to this person, you will be safe."

4.   To nurture subordinates, be careful not to divide or push too hard for their path to be right.

5.   If you show an attitude of listening carefully to subordinates and business partners, subordinates will not be discouraged.

Type 9: Peacemaker
(Wish harmony and peace)

1.   He has a comprehensive perspective, is calm and stable, so he can skillfully summarize various opinions.

2.   He is a good listener, accepts the feelings of subordinates and is able to encourage them.

3.   He is overly optimistic and ignores problems or delays his response.

4.   He leaves his subordinates alone too much; they need important and precise guidance.

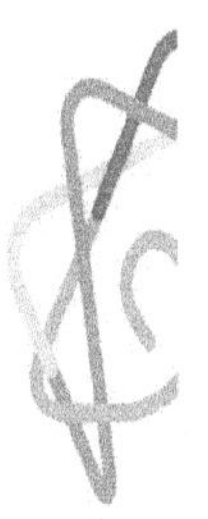

APPENDIX II

Bibliography

Abraham, K, Leonard y Virginia Woolf. (1965). Selected Papers on Psychoanalysis. London, Hoghart Press.

Chestnut, B. (2013). The Complete Enneagram: 27 Paths to Greater Self-Knowledge.

Everett, Daniel. (2014). No duermas, hay serpientes. Madrid, Turner.

Field, Syd (2002). Screenplay: The Foundations of Screenwriting.

Gurdjieff, G. I. The Enneagram.

Horney, K. (1990). Neurosis and Human Growth (New York, W.W. Norton Co.

Klein, M. (1988). Envidia y Gratitud. Ed. Paidos, Barcelona.

McKee, Robert. (1997). Story, Substance, Structure, Style and the Principles of Screenwriting.

Naranjo, C. (1994). Character and Neurosis, Gateways/DHHB, Nevada City (California).

Palmer, H. (2014). El Eneagrama. Barcelona: La liebre de marzo.

Riso, Don Richard y Russ Hudson. (2000). La Sabiduría del Eneagrama. Ediciones Urano.

Shapiro, D. (1989). Psychotherapy ofNeurotic Character. New York, Basic Books.

Sheldon, W.H., (1942). The Varieties of Temperament. New York, Harper Brothers.

Snyder, Blake. (2005). Save the Cat!

Steiner, C. (1985). Scripts People Play. New York, Bantam Books.

Tart, C. T. (1975). Transpersonal Psychologies.

Truby, John. (2007). The Anatomy of Story.

Contact Links

Where do you buy other books by the author?

Social networking:

https://www.facebook.com/ElConstructordelasLetras

@MazueraCarlos

Instagram
@escritormazuera

Carlos Mazuera

Email

asturiaspluma@gmail.com

Other books by the author:

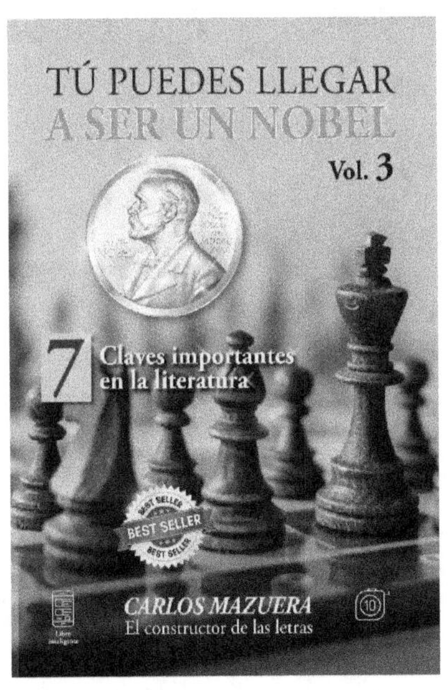

TÚ PUEDES LLEGAR
A SER UN NOBEL
Vol. 3
7
Claves importantes
en la literatura
BEST SELLER
CARLOS MAZUERA
El constructor de las letras

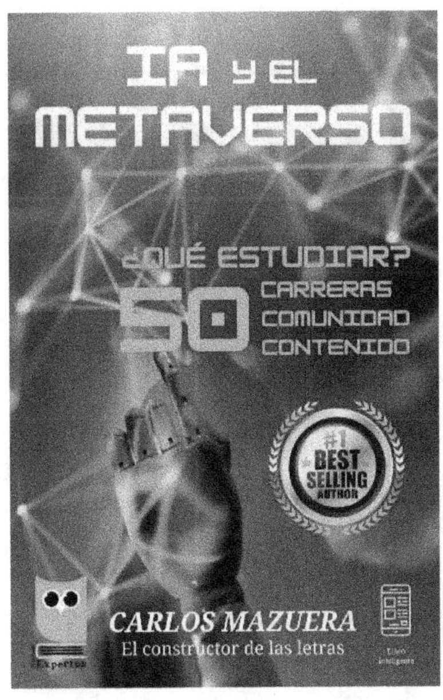

IA Y EL
METAVERSO
¿QUÉ ESTUDIAR?
50
CARRERAS
COMUNIDAD
CONTENIDO
BEST SELLING AUTHOR
CARLOS MAZUERA
El constructor de las letras

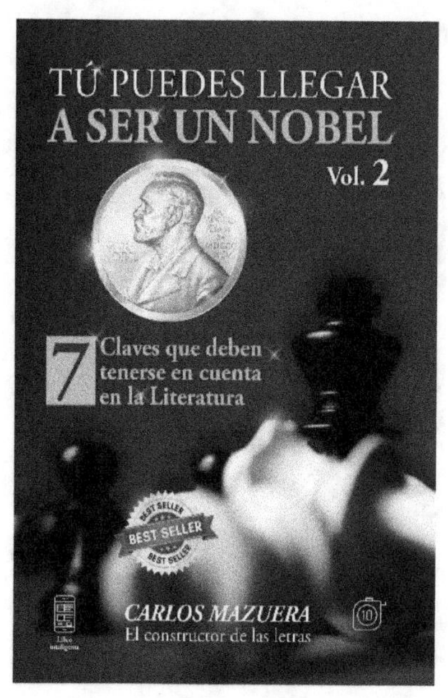
TÚ PUEDES LLEGAR
A SER UN NOBEL
Vol. 2
7 Claves que deben tenerse en cuenta en la Literatura
BEST SELLER
BEST SELLER
BEST SELLER
CARLOS MAZUERA
El constructor de las letras
Libro inteligente

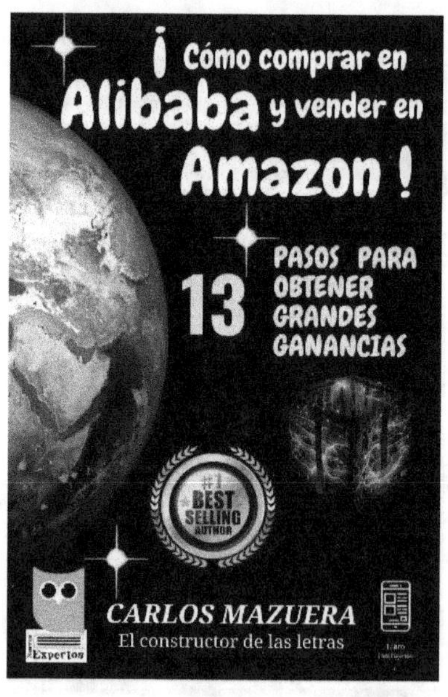
¡ Cómo comprar en
Alibaba y vender en
Amazon !
13 PASOS PARA OBTENER GRANDES GANANCIAS
#1 BEST SELLING AUTHOR
CARLOS MAZUERA
El constructor de las letras
Expertos
Libro inteligente

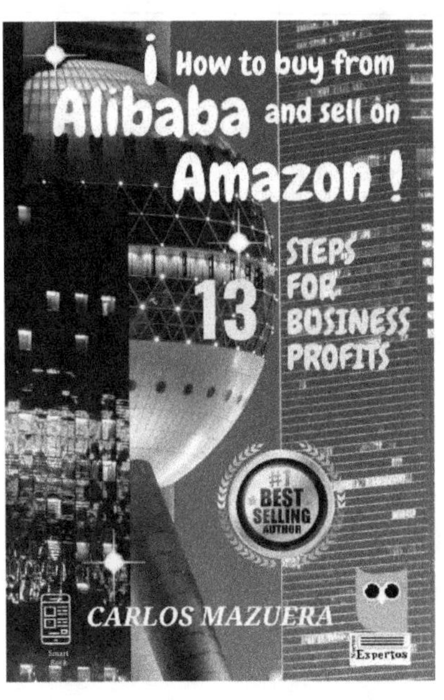
¡ How to buy from
Alibaba and sell on
Amazon !
13
STEPS
FOR
BUSINESS
PROFITS
#1
BEST
SELLING
AUTHOR
CARLOS MAZUERA
Expertos

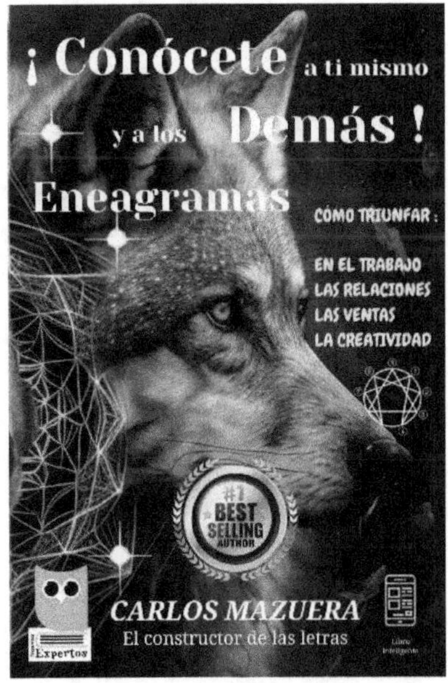
¡ Conócete a ti mismo
y a los Demás !
Eneagramas
CÓMO TRIUNFAR :
EN EL TRABAJO
LAS RELACIONES
LAS VENTAS
LA CREATIVIDAD
#1
BEST
SELLING
AUTHOR
CARLOS MAZUERA
El constructor de las letras
Expertos

* 9 7 8 9 9 6 2 1 7 8 1 7 0 *